BRIOCHE
Knit
LOVE

21 Skill Building Projects from Simple to Sublime

Michele Lee Bernstein

PDXKnitterati

Library House Press

Library House Press

First Published in 2021 by
Library House Press
2195 Hyacinth St NE #106
Salem, OR 97301
www.libraryhousepress.com

ISBN-13: 978-1-7361101-2-6

10 9 8 7 6 5 4 3 2 1

Library of Congress Control Number: 2021917862

Cover and book design by Carlee Wright for Library House Press
Photography by Angela Watts of Tekoa Rose Photography
Tutorial photography by Marie Greene

Printed and bound in the United States.

For Phil Bernstein,
my sweetheart and biggest fan.

And for my Aunt Rose,
who taught me how to knit.

Contents

INTRODUCTION..6

CHAPTER 1: 9
Getting Started with Brioche Knitting
  Basic Brioche Stitches.................................10

CHAPTER 2..15
One-Color Brioche Knitting
  Hello Brioche Scarf....................................16
  Hello Brioche Hats, Aran and Worsted...................19
  Hello Brioche Mitts....................................21

CHAPTER 3..23
Two-Color Brioche Knitting, In the Round
  Grande Brioche Cowl....................................26
  Peppermint Mocha Cup Cozy..............................28
  Iced Latte Cowl..30

CHAPTER 4..33
Two-Color Brioche Knitting, Flat
  Italian Soda Cowl......................................34
  Peppermint Mocha Coaster...............................37

CHAPTER 5..39
Syncopated Brioche
  Crema Cowl...40
  Shortbread Scarf.......................................43
  Chocolate Chip Shortbread (recipe)....................47

CHAPTER 6..48
Brioche Increases and Decreases
  Tutorials..49
  Iced Latte Hat...60
  Berry Galette Cowl.....................................64
  Berry Galette Wristlets................................68
  Green Tea Chai Scarf...................................72
  Latte Leaf Coaster and Cup Cozy........................76

CHAPTER 7..84
Putting it All Together
  Cappuccino Cowl..85
  Seafoam Latte Scarf....................................90
  Seagull Flight Shawl...................................94
  Coffee Bean Trivia Cowl...............................101
  Coffee Breakers Cowl/Shawl............................107

CHAPTER 8...114
Fixing Mistakes

CHAPTER 9...117
Special Techniques

ABBREVIATIONS...119
RESOURCES...121
ACKNOWLEDGEMENTS..123
THANK YOU...125
ABOUT THE AUTHOR 127
INDEX...128

Introduction

When I was 14, I spent the summer with my Aunt Rose and her family in southern California. Aunt Rose loves to knit; she wanted to share that joy with me. We went to her local yarn shop to choose a pattern and yarn. My first knitting project was a baby blue wool pullover, knit in the round, with cables up the front. It was beautiful! But...we didn't do a gauge swatch, and my sweater was enormous. I loved knitting it, but I didn't wear it much.

Many years later, I decided to shrink that sweater. I washed it in the washing machine with hot water. Success! Kind of. Did you know that knitting shrinks more in length than in width? The resulting sweater was a very short, very boxy pullover, with a neck opening that was too small for my head.

I've learned a lot about knitting since then: I love simple knitting with a dash of technique to keep things interesting, and I love designing accessories. It turns out that I have a two-skein attention span for most knitting; halfway through I'm already dreaming about the next project. Plus, three of my favorite words are: gauge not critical. Accessories don't have to fit the same way sweaters do, and I'm not afraid to make the most of that. Clearly, I learned a few valuable lessons from that first ill-fitting sweater!

In 2017, I tried brioche knitting for the first time. Brioche had been on my bucket list for several years, so I finally took a class. In just three hours, we covered flat, two-color brioche with several selvage options, and increases and decreases, too. It was a fun class that piqued my interest, but when I returned home, I put it away for a few months before picking it up again.

When I finally came back to brioche knitting, I had completely forgotten everything I learned in class. I decided to start over – from the very beginning. A bit of internet research convinced me that two-color Brioche Rib in the round would be a great starting point, and I ran with it. I loved the results so much that I turned that first project into a pattern, and, with it, I've taught hundreds of knitters the first steps of brioche knitting. (You can find that first pattern, Petite Brioche, for free on my website at PDXKnitterati.com.)

After Petite Brioche, I tackled brioche increases, decreases and syncopated brioche. Each technique added more variety and interest (and allowed me to create such pretty patterns!). Learning these techniques one at a time allowed each skill to build upon the one before. The result? I've fallen in love with brioche!

Let's go on this brioche journey together, shall we? I'll teach you brioche knitting the same way I taught myself: one skill at a time. We'll begin with the basics and - little by little - we'll move through new skills and advanced techniques. We'll meet in a virtual café to learn the basic brioche stitches for one-color and two-color brioche, both in the round and flat. We'll move on to increasing, decreasing and syncopated brioche. Finally, we'll put everything together and escape with our brioche for coffee at my beloved Oregon Coast, a source of endless inspiration. Come knit with me!

Michele Lee Bernstein

CHAPTER 1

Getting Started with Brioche Knitting

This book takes you through the basics of brioche knitting with small, approachable patterns. They're the perfect size for learning new things. You can check out each new technique to see if it's your cup of tea... or coffee. Gauge is not critical for success for most of these accessories, which means you can concentrate on just learning something new. Yarns vary a bit within the categories of worsted weight or fingering weight; your yarn may require bigger or smaller needles to get a fabric that makes you happy. If your gauge is not exactly the same as mine, your project may require more or less yarn, and the result may be a bit larger or smaller.

CHOOSING YOUR SUPPLIES

I love big yarn for teaching knitting. It's much easier to learn when you can really see your stitches. For that reason, most of the beginning projects in this book are knit with worsted weight wool yarn. I've saved the patterns using fingering weight yarn for the last chapter when you'll be ready to use your new skills.

Choose a yarn that isn't too slippery when you're just starting; it will help if you drop a stitch. Wool yarns with a bit of "grab" (i.e. rustic) can also help keep your fabric from stretching lengthwise. Non-superwash wools are a good choice if you're knitting a long scarf. For smaller projects, like hats and cowls, where fabric weight and stretching aren't as much of an issue, superwash wool yarns are fine.

Other than the very first pattern, all of the patterns in this book require circular or double pointed needles, even for brioche knit flat. Flat two-color brioche rib requires sliding back to the beginning of the row to work the second color, and you can't do that with straight needles. When knitting brioche in the round, I recommend circular needles in a standard length appropriate for your project. You could also use magic loop, two circulars, or double pointed needles, but using a circular needle in the right length means you won't be struggling to locate your yarn overs at the ends of the needles on your first projects. For small circumference projects or closing the top of a hat, you'll eventually need one of those other methods, but let's start as simply as we can.

Brioche knitting is very stretchy because of the extra yarn in the stitches, and because it is a ribbed fabric. You'll want to use needles a bit smaller than you'd expect for your worsted weight projects. On the other hand, for your fingering weight projects, you may need a slightly larger needle so that your fabric has the desired drape. Let your yarn be your guide.

Stitch markers are helpful for keeping track of your beginning of round and pattern repeats. A row counter is also very handy.

BEFORE YOU START KNITTING

Abbreviations are listed on page 119. Special techniques for blocking, casting on, and binding off are covered in Chapter 9 on page 117. Take time to read the tips in each chapter; they'll apply to most of your brioche knitting.

BASIC BRIOCHE STITCHES

Brioche Rib is a dense, extra squishy fabric. It is created by slipping every other stitch; a yarn over is added to each slipped stitch. On the following row or round, the slipped stitch is knit or purled together (as appropriate) with its paired yarn over, and the stitches that were worked on the previous row or round are slipped and given a yarn over. It takes two passes for all the stitches to be worked. The yarn over is not a separate stitch on its own; the slipped stitch and yarn over are one stitch unit.

Brioche Rib is a reversible fabric. Two-color Brioche Rib looks the same on both sides, with the colors reversed.

brk: brioche knit

Knit the stitch with its paired yarn over.

brp: brioche purl

Purl the stitch with its paired yarn over.

sl1yo: slip 1 yarn over

Slip the stitch purlwise, and give it a yarn over before the following stitch. The yarn must be at the front of your work before slipping; this is so the right leg of the yo will be at the front of your needle, just like your slipped stitch. This looks different depending on whether the next stitch is a brk or a brp.

TIP The sl1yo is also used on setup rows at the beginning of your project; it's made the same way between knit or purl stitches as the sl1yo between brk or brp stitches.

sl1yo, brk: English, American, throwing

Yarn is in back after working previous brk. Bring yarn between needles to front of work and slip the next st purlwise.

Insert right needle into next st and its paired yo. Bring yarn over right needle.

Brk the stitch.

Completed sl1yo, brk. Slipped stitch has a paired yarn over, and yarn is in back after brk. The slipped stitch and its paired yarn over are *one unit*, the yarn over is not a separate stitch.

See Resources on page 121 for additional assistance.

sl1yo, brp: English, American, throwing

Yarn is in front after working previous brp. Slip the next stitch purlwise.

Bring yarn over right needle and down between your needles to the front (making the yo).

Brp the next stitch.

Completed sl1yo, brp. Slipped stitch has a paired yo, and yarn is in front after brp. The slipped stitch and its paired yarn over are *one unit*, the yarn over is not a separate stitch.

sl1yo, brk: Continental, picking

Yarn is in back after working previous brk.

Duck right needle behind yarn and slip the next stitch purlwise.

Brk the next stitch.

Completed sl1yo, brk. Slipped stitch has a paired yarn over, and yarn is in back after brk. The slipped stitch and its paired yarn over are *one unit*, the yarn over is not a separate stitch.

See Resources on page 121 for additional assistance.

sl1yo, brp: Continental, picking

Yarn is in front after working previous brp. Slip the next stitch purlwise.

Bring yarn over right needle and down between the needles to the front (making the yo).

Brp the next stitch.

Completed sl1yo, brp. Slipped stitch has a paired yo, and yarn is in front after brp. The slipped stitch and its paired yarn over are *one unit*, the yarn over is not a separate stitch.

CHAPTER 2

One-Color Brioche Knitting

Portland, Oregon, my hometown, is a city of coffee lovers. Cafes are great places to meet up with a friend for a little knitting and conversation. Coffee is great with brioche; sometimes the brioche is knitting, and sometimes it's pastry. If I'm lucky, there's some of both!

Pour yourself a coffee and let's get started with one-color brioche. Your first project is a flat brioche scarf, knit with super bulky yarn. Then we'll knit a hat to learn about knitting brioche in the round. Finally, we'll end this chapter with fingerless mitts that are knit in the round, and flat, and in the round again. Magic! All of these designs share the name Hello Brioche.

TECHNIQUES/TIPS FOR KNITTING BRIOCHE

The sl1yo is the heart of brioche knitting. Your yarn needs to be at the front of your work before beginning the sl1yo, so the stitch mount of your yarn over matches the stitch mount of the slipped stitch, right leg forward. If you're on a brioche knit row or round, you'll need to bring your yarn between your needles to the front of your work before slipping for your sl1yo. If you're on a brioche purl row or round, the yarn is already at the front of your work, so you'll slip the stitch and then give it the yarn over.

Read all the tips in the tip boxes in this chapter, even if you're not knitting all the projects; they'll give you hints for all of your brioche knitting.

Hello Brioche Scarf

The Hello Brioche Scarf is a perfect introduction to one-color brioche rib. It's knit flat with super bulky weight yarn, so you can easily see your stitches. And it's quick! This rib pattern has no purl stitches; so you're learning brioche with half the work.

YARN

Super bulky weight yarn | Shown in Malabrigo Rasta (100% Merino Wool, 90 yards/82 meters in 150g), 1 Skein Arco Iris | 90 yards/82 meters

NEEDLES

US 15/10.0 mm straight or circular needles, or size to attain fabric you like

GAUGE

7 sts in 4"/10 cm in Brioche Rib, worked flat, before blocking

NOTIONS

Tapestry needle

FINISHED SIZE

5.5"/14 cm wide x 31"/79 cm long unblocked. I like this size and loftiness, so I didn't block mine. You can steam block if you'd like to relax the fabric a bit, and wet block if you want it to be longer. Wet blocking would make it up to 40"/101.5 cm in length, and 5"/12.5 cm in width.

DIRECTIONS: KNIT VERSION

CO 12 sts using Long Tail Cast On.

Setup Row: *K1, sl1yo; rep from * to last 2 sts, k1, sl1 purlwise wyif.

BRIOCHE RIB

Row 1 and all rows: K1, *sl1yo, brk; rep from * to last st, sl1 purlwise wyif.

Rep Row 1 until work measures 31"/79 cm or desired length. I worked until there was just enough yarn (20"/51 cm) to bind off.

FINISHING

Bind off in rib pattern, working brk into the sl1yos and p the single purl sts.

Sew in ends. Steam or wet block as desired, or don't block at all if you are happy with it as is.

Are you disappointed you didn't get to learn to brioche purl? Surprise! Turn the page and you can knit this again with with brioche purl, or move on to the next project.

DIRECTIONS: PURL VERSION

CO 12 sts using Long Tail Cast On.

Setup Row: *P1, sl1yo; rep from * to last 2 sts, p1, sl1 purlwise wyib.

BRIOCHE RIB

Row 1 and all rows: P1, *sl1yo, brp; rep from * to last st, sl1 purlwise wyib.

Rep Row 1 until work measures 31"/79 cm or desired length. Bind off in rib pattern, working brp into the sl1yos and k the single knit sts (row begins with p1).

Sew in ends. Steam or wet block as desired, or don't block at all if you are happy with it as is.

Hello Brioche Scarf, Knit Version. (Purl version looks the same!)

Hello Brioche Hat

The Hello Brioche Hat is the next step in your brioche adventure. This one-color hat is knit in the round from the bottom up. You can knit it in Aran weight or worsted weight yarn. Aran weight is, of course, quicker and squooshier!

TIP Brioche rib is very stretchy. You'll want to allow about 3 - 4"/7.5 - 10 cm of negative ease. For example, my Aran weight hat is 19"/48.5 cm in circumference, unstretched, and it is roomy on my 22"/56 cm head.

YARN

Aran version: Aran weight yarn | Shown in Knit Picks Muse (100% Superwash Merino, 114 yards/104 meters in 100g), 1 skein Dreamy | 110 yards/101 meters for largest size

Worsted version: Worsted weight yarn | Shown in Malabrigo Rios (100% Superwash Merino Wool, 210 yards/192 meters in 100 g), 1 skein Indiecita | 190 yards/174 meters for largest size

NEEDLES

US 8/5.0 mm 16"/40 cm circular needle for Aran weight, or US 6/4.0 mm 16"/40 cm circular needle for worsted weight, or size to attain gauge. Gauge-size double pointed needles or additional circular, or long circular for magic loop to close top of hat.

GAUGE

Aran: 14 st in 4"/10 cm in Brioche Rib worked in the round, after blocking, unstretched

Worsted: 16 st in 4"/10 cm in Brioche Rib worked in the round, after blocking, unstretched

NOTIONS

Tapestry needle
Stitch marker to denote beginning of round

FINISHED SIZE

Small (Medium, Large)

Aran: 17 (18, 19)"/43 (46, 48) cm circumference, 6 (6.5, 7)"/15 (16.5, 18) cm tall

Worsted: 17 (18, 19)"/43 (46, 48) cm circumference, 6 (6.5, 7)"/15 (16.5, 18) cm tall

Hello Brioche Hats in worsted weight (left) and Aran weight (right) yarn

Hello Brioche Hat in worsted weight yarn

DIRECTIONS

CO 60 (64, 68) sts for Aran hat, 68 (72, 76) sts for worsted hat, using Long Tail Cast On. PM, join to work in the round. Knit 5 rounds.

Setup Rnd 1: *K1, sl1yo; rep from * to end.
Setup Rnd 2: *Sl1yo, brp; rep from * to end.

TIP Brk round (and Setup Rnd 1) ends with sl1yo; next round begins with sl1yo, brp. Yes, a sl1yo on each side of the marker. Just make sure each stitch has its paired yo, and you're set!

TIP Brp round (and Setup Rnd 2) ends with brp; next round begins with brk, sl1yo.

BRIOCHE RIB

Rnd 1: *Brk, sl1yo; rep from * to end.
Rnd 2: *Sl1yo, brp; rep from * to end.

Rep Rnds 1 and 2 until work measures 6 (6.5, 7)"/15 (16.5, 18) cm from the cast on edge, or desired height, ending with Rnd 2. Crown shaping is quick and flat, no height added.

CROWN SHAPING

Rnd 1: Brk, *brk2tog (knit the p st and the following sl1yo all together); rep from * to last st, remove marker, k2tog (last st of rnd and first st from next rnd) , replace marker. 30 (32, 34) st rem for Aran hat, 34 (36, 38) sts rem for worsted hat.

Rnd 2: *K2tog; rep from * to end. 15 (16, 17) sts rem for Aran hat, 17 (18, 19) st rem for worsted hat.

Rnd 3: *K2tog; rep from * to last st, k1. (Medium size will not have last k1.) 8 (8, 9) sts rem for Aran hat, 9 (9, 10) st rem for worsted hat.

FINISHING

Cut yarn leaving 6"/15 cm tail, pass yarn through remaining stitches twice and cinch tightly. Sew in ends. Steam or wet block.

Hello Brioche Mitts

The Hello Brioche Mitts give you a chance to work Brioche Rib both flat and in the round. They begin in the round at the wrist. The thumb hole is worked back and forth (flat), and then you'll go back to knitting in the round to complete the palm of the mitt. The mitts are shown with a 3"/7.5 cm cuff, but you can make the cuffs and palm longer or shorter to suit your fancy.

TIP Brioche Rib is very stretchy; you'll want to have zero or negative ease for these mitts. Make them the same measurement as around the base of your fingers, closest to your palm.

YARN
Worsted weight yarn | Shown in Malabrigo Washted (100% Superwash Merino Wool, 210 yards/192 meters in 100 g), 1 skein Arco Iris | 125 yards/114 meters for largest size

NEEDLES
US 6/4.0 mm double pointed needles, or 2 circulars, or long circular for magic loop, or size to attain gauge.

GAUGE
16 sts and 24 rows in 4"/10 cm in Brioche Rib worked flat, after blocking, unstretched. Always count after finishing a Row/Round 2.

NOTIONS
Tapestry needle
Stitch marker to denote beginning of round, if beginning of round is not at end of needle

FINISHED SIZE
Small (Medium, Large)

6 (7, 8)"/15 (18, 20) cm circumference, 7.5 (7.5, 8)"/19 (19, 20) cm tall

Hello Brioche Mitts

DIRECTIONS

WRIST, WORKED IN THE ROUND
Loosely CO 24 (28, 32) sts using Long Tail Cast On. PM, join to work in the round. Knit 1 round. (Note: I leave space between sts when casting on, so it's not tight.)

TIP Having the beginning/end of round at the end of your needle can be confusing, because your last yo can fall off the end of the needle. If it's too annoying, shift your stitches so the beginning/end of round is in the middle of a needle instead. You can place a marker there as a reminder.

Setup Rnd 1: *K1, sl1yo; rep from * to end.
Setup Rnd 2: *Sl1yo, brp; rep from * to end.

BRIOCHE RIB

Rnd 1: *Brk, sl1yo; rep from * to end.
Rnd 2: *Sl1yo, brp; rep from * to end.

Rep Rnds 1 and 2 until work measures 3"/7.5 cm or desired length for wrist, ending with a Rnd 2.

THUMB OPENING, WORKED FLAT

Row 1 (RS): *Brk, sl1yo; rep from * to last 2 sts, brk, sl1 purlwise wyif. Turn work.

Row 2: K1, *sl1yo, brk; rep from * to last st, sl1 wyif. Turn.

Rep Row 2 on RS and WS until the thumb opening measures 2"/5 cm tall, ending with a WS row.

PALM, WORKED IN THE ROUND

Setup Rnd 1: K1, *sl1yo, brk; rep from * to last st, sl1yo. Join to work in the round again to begin next rnd. Snug yarn up after first 2 sts of next 2 rnds to avoid gaps at the top of your thumb opening.

Setup Rnd 2: *Sl1yo, brp; rep from * to end.

Rep Rnds 1 and 2 of Brioche Rib (same as at wrist) until work measures 7.5 (7.5, 8)"/19 (19, 20) cm from CO edge, or desired height, ending with Rnd 2.

FINISHING

BO in rib pattern using Suspended Bind Off (see Special Techniques), working brk into the sl1yos and p the single purl stitches. Sew in ends. Steam block.

Hello Brioche Mitts

CHAPTER 3

Two-Color Brioche Knitting, In the Round

One-color brioche is lovely and squishy, but two-color brioche is where this stitch really shines. When someone says "brioche knitting," this is generally what you envision. Two-color Brioche Rib is a reversible fabric, and each side highlights one of the two colors. I think it's easier to learn two-color brioche in the round first, because the right side of the work is always facing you. All of the brioche knit rounds are worked with one color, and all of the brioche purl rounds are worked with the other color. Simple!

TECHNIQUES/TIPS FOR KNITTING TWO-COLOR BRIOCHE IN THE ROUND

Read all the tips in the tip boxes in this chapter, even if you're not knitting all the projects. They'll give you hints for all your brioche knitting.

> **TIP** I usually use the lighter color (LC) for the brk rounds, and darker color (DC) for brp rounds. Light colors seem to advance toward us, and dark colors recede. Using the lighter color as your featured color makes your brioche pop!

The one tricky place with two-color brioche in the round is the transition between rounds. Here are a couple of ways to handle it. Note: Always drop the old yarn in front when a round is complete regardless of which method you use, unless otherwise directed.

Method 1: Lock in that yarn over! This is how I usually work brioche in the round.

Last 2 sts of LC brk rnd: Brk, slip last st, complete the yo by taking the yarn over the RH needle and then between the needles to the front. Drop LC in front and to the right of your needles, sm, pick up DC from front where you previously left it (don't twist yarns around each other), begin next round with sl1yo, brp. You have a sl1yo at end of the old round next to a sl1yo at beginning of the new round.

Last st of DC brp rnd: Brp, drop DC in front and to the right of your needles, move LC between needles from front to back, sm, begin next rnd with brk, sl1yo. You have a brp at the end of the old round next to brk at the beginning of the new round.

Method 2: Delayed yo. This method is good when you're working with dpns or 2 circulars, and there's no way to lock in the last yo at the end of the needle on the brk rnd. It also works when you forgot to lock in that last LC yo when using Method 1.

Last 2 sts of LC brk rnd: Brk, slip last st, drop LC in front between last 2 sts (do not complete the yo), sm, pick up DC from front where you previously left it (don't twist yarns around each other), begin sl1yo, brp of next rnd. You have a slipped st at end of the old round next to a sl1yo at the beginning of the new round. Last st of old round is missing its yarn over; you'll add it at the end of the next round. Look forward to "delayed" gratification!

Last st of DC brp rnd: Lift LC over left needle to use as yo when making brp in last st. After final brp is complete drop LC in back and DC in front, sm, use LC from back to begin next rnd with brk, sl1yo. You have a brp at the end of the old round next to brk at the beginning of the new round.

TIP Don't stop at the marker; it's confusing to pick up your project and not know which of the two yarns is the working yarn. Stop somewhere else in your work. The single working yarn between your needles tells you if you're working a lighter color (LC) or darker color (DC) round.

TIP The yo is the opposite color of the stitch you are slipping.

TIP Brioche Rib doesn't look like ribbing until round 5 or 6. Don't give up too early!

Grande Brioche Cowl

Brioche buns are buttery and delicious; they're the perfect cross between bread and pastry. But wait…we're here for the knitting, right? I adore brioche knitting as much (or more) than the buns, and things are about to get extra delicious in this cowl.

I've been teaching two-color brioche in the round for years using my Petite Brioche headband pattern, but this aptly named Grande Brioche Cowl takes that early idea a bit further. It's an upsized version of the original that results in a project you can wear all winter long. (To make cowl wider or narrower, adjust cast on by a multiple of 2 stitches.)

I love the way stockinette stitch rolls when it's left to its own devices – it creates a simple and stylish tubular edge, which is perfect for this scrumptious cowl.

YARN

Worsted weight yarn in 2 contrasting colors | Shown in Malabrigo Rios (100% Superwash Wool, 210 yards/192 meters in 100 g), 1 skein each color Azules (DC) and Aquamarine (LC) | 95 yards/87 meters DC and 75 yards/69 meters LC

NEEDLES

US 6/4.0 mm 16"/40 cm circular needle, or size to attain gauge or a fabric you like

GAUGE

18 sts in 4"/10 cm in Brioche Rib worked in the round, after blocking | Gauge not critical

NOTIONS

Tapestry needle
Stitch marker to denote beginning of round

FINISHED SIZE

20"/51 cm circumference, 5.5"/14 cm tall, size adjustable

DIRECTIONS

With DC, CO 92 sts using Long Tail Cast On. PM, join to work in the round. Knit 6 rounds.

Setup Rnd 1 (LC): Join LC. *K1, sl1yo; rep from * to end.
Setup Rnd 2 (DC): *Sl1yo, brp; rep from * to end.

BRIOCHE RIB

Rnd 1 (LC): *Brk, sl1yo; rep from * to end.

Rnd 2 (DC): *Sl1yo, brp; rep from * to end.

Rep Rnds 1 and 2 until Brioche Rib section measures 4.5"/11 cm or desired total cowl height minus .5"/1 cm, ending with a Rnd 2. Cut LC, leaving 6"/15 cm tail.

Closing Rnd (DC): *Brk, k1; rep from * to end.

Knit 5 more rnds.

FINISHING

BO all sts knitwise using Suspended Bind Off (see Special Techniques). Sew in ends. Steam or wet block.

Peppermint Mocha Cup Cozy

Here's a fun fact: Brioche knitting doesn't have to be Brioche Rib. The Peppermint Mocha Cup Cozy is knit in stockinette brioche, a versatile option for changing-up your brioche game.

I've said that gauge is not critical for most of the projects in this book, but you'll want to make sure your cup cozy isn't too loose for your cup. Slippery cups of hot coffee are not the goal here! You can either adjust your cozy by needle size, or by changing the cast on by a multiple of 2 stitches. This cozy is knit in the round from the bottom up.

See the Peppermint Mocha Coaster pattern on page 37 for the matching coaster. Make a set, or two, or more!

YARN

Worsted weight yarn in 2 contrasting colors | Shown in Malabrigo Rios (100% Superwash Wool, 210 yards/192 meters in 100 g), 1 skein each color English Rose (DC) and Almond Blossom (LC) | 16 yards/15 meters DC and 12 yards/11 meters LC for each cup cozy

NEEDLES

US 5/3.75 mm set of 4 or 5 dpns or 2 circular needles or one 32"/80 cm circular for magic loop to work small circumference, or size to attain gauge

GAUGE

15 sts and 24 rows in 4"/10 cm in stockinette brioche worked in the round, after steam blocking

NOTIONS

Tapestry needle
Stitch marker to denote beginning of round (optional, depending on where you put your beginning of round)

FINISHED SIZE

8.5"/22 cm circumference, 2.5"/6 cm tall

DIRECTIONS

With DC, CO 32 sts using Long Tail Cast On. PM, join to work in the round. Knit 1 round.

Setup Rnd 1 (LC): Join LC. *K1, sl1yo; rep from * to end. Drop LC at front of work without creating the final yo; it will hang between last 2 sts of rnd. All LC rnds end this way. Last st of rnd is missing its yo; it will get its yo at end of next rnd.

Setup Rnd 2 (DC): *Sl1yo, brk; rep from * to end. To brk the last st, lift LC over left needle; this is the missing yo from previous rnd. Brk into this st and its yo. Drop DC in back of work. All DC rnds end this way. Pick up LC and begin next rnd.

STOCKINETTE BRIOCHE

Rnd 1 (LC): *Brk, sl1yo; rep from * to end.
Rnd 2 (DC): *Sl1yo, brk; rep from * to end.

Rep Rnds 1 and 2 until work measures 2.5"/6 cm or desired height, ending with a Rnd 2. Move LC to back between the needles, cut LC, leaving 6"/15 cm tail.

FINISHING

Closing Rnd (DC): *Brk, k1; rep from * to end.

BO all sts loosely knitwise using Suspended Bind Off. Sew in ends. Steam block.

Iced Latte Cowl

The Iced Latte Cowl is a gentle introduction to two-color brioche. Brioche Rib and Garter Stitch share the same row gauge, so they can be combined for pleasing results. The checkerboard-effect of brioche and garter stitch reminds me of chilly ice cubes in a summer latte!

The Iced Latte Cowl is worked in the round from the bottom up. Adjust the width of your project by adding or subtracting stitches in multiples of 12, and knit to your desired height.

See the Iced Latte Hat pattern on page 60 for the coordinating hat.

YARN

DK weight yarn in 2 contrasting colors | Shown in Hazel Knits Lively DK (90% Superwash Merino, 10% nylon, 275 yards/252 meters in 130 g), 1 skein each color Iris (DC) and Cackle (LC) | 170 yards/155 meters DC and 140 yards/128 meters LC

NEEDLES

US 5/3.75 mm 24"/60 cm circular needle, or size to attain gauge or a fabric you like | US 7/4.5 mm 24"/60 cm circular needle for final edging and bind off

GAUGE

19 sts in 4"/10 cm in Iced Latte Stitch worked in the round, after light steam blocking | Gauge not critical

NOTIONS

Tapestry needle
Stitch markers

FINISHED SIZE

36"/91 cm circumference, 7"/18 cm tall

DIRECTIONS

With DC and smaller needle, loosely CO 168 sts using Long Tail Cast On. (To make the cowl wider or narrower, adjust cast on by multiples of 12 stitches.) PM, join to work in the rnd. Knit 1 rnd. Continue with smaller needle. Work Setup Rnds and Iced Latte Stitch from written instructions or chart. (See chart on next page.)

Setup Rnd 1 (DC): *K6, (k1, sl1yo) 3x, pm; rep from * to end (a final marker will not be placed at the end of round as the BOR marker is already in place). After last sl1yo, leave DC in front. All DC rnds end with yarn in front. From here on, slip markers as you come to them.

Setup Rnd 2 (LC): *K6, (sl1yo, brk) 3x; rep from * to end. Leave LC yarn in back. All LC rnds end with yarn in back.

ICED LATTE STITCH

Worked over 12 sts and 24 rounds

Rnds 1, 3, 5, 7, 9 (DC): *P6, (brp, sl1yo) 3x; rep from * to end.

Rnds 2, 4, 6, 8, 10 (LC): *K6, (sl1yo, brk) 3x; rep from * to end.

Rnd 11 (DC): *(P1, sl1yo) 3x, (brp, p1) 3x; rep from * to end.

Rnd 12 (LC): *(Sl1yo, brk) 3x, k6; rep from * to end.

ICED LATTE STITCH CHART

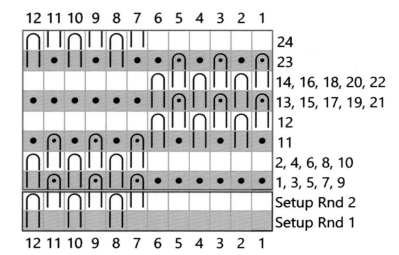

KEY

☐	knit
⬚•	purl
∩	brk
⋒	brp
‖	sl1yo
☐	Setup rnds
☐	Pattern Repeat
▨	DC rnds
☐	LC rnds

Rnds 13, 15, 17, 19, 21 (DC): *(Brp, sl1yo) 3x, p6; rep from * to end.

Rnds 14, 16, 18, 20, 22 (LC): *(Sl1yo, brk) 3x, k6; rep from * to end.

Rnd 23 (DC): *(Brp, p1) 3x, (p1, sl1yo) 3x; rep from * to end.

Rnd 24 (LC): *K6, (sl1yo, brk) 3x; rep from * to end.

Rep Rnds 1 – 24 of Iced Latte Stitch pattern to desired height, ending with Rnd 21 (DC) or Rnd 9 (DC).

Cowl shown has 3 reps of Iced Latte Stitch pattern (excluding last Rnds 22 – 24).

LC Closing Rnd if you ended with Rnd 9: *K6, (k1, brk) 3x; rep to end. Cut LC, leaving 6"/15 cm tail.

LC Closing Rnd if you ended with Rnd 21: *(K1, brk) 3x, k6; rep to end. Cut LC, leaving 6"/15 cm tail.

Edging (DC): Using larger needle, knit all sts.

FINISHING

Using larger needle, BO all sts knitwise using Suspended Bind Off to provide flexible edge.

Sew in ends. Lightly steam block.

CHAPTER 4

Two-Color Brioche Knitting, Flat

I prefer to teach two-color flat brioche *after* teaching two-color brioche in the round. When you work brioche flat, one color will represent the brioche knits on the right side of your knitting, and the brioche purls on the wrong side, and vice versa for your other color. To keep things straight, you'll need to mind your Ps and Qs. Or knits and purls.

TECHNIQUES/TIPS FOR KNITTING BRIOCHE FLAT

Two-color flat brioche knitting requires two passes for each numbered row; you're working half the stitches each time, and slipping every other stitch. Odd numbered rows are usually RS rows; even numbered rows are usually WS rows. Work Row 1 with your first color, then *slide* work back to the other end of needle to work Row 1 with your second color across the same side of the work. After these first RS rows are complete, *turn* the work, and work Row 2 with your first color and then second color before turning work again.

TIP I use yf and yb to tell you where your yarn should be; move it between your needles to the front or back of your work. It's just an extra hint; even if it's not stated, you'd have to move the yarn to the front or back to be able to purl or knit the following stitch.

TIP If your yarns are at the same end of a row, you're ready to turn your work. If the yarns are at opposite ends of the row, slide back to the beginning so the second yarn can catch up to the first yarn. I also tell you when to slide, and when to turn, as another extra hint.

Italian Soda Cowl

Italian Soda is a reversible buttoned cowl, knit flat. Is one side better than the other? That's your call! I serendipitously found out that adding a twist before buttoning means you can see both sides at once, in colorful sparkling conversation with each other!

I'm calling the two yarns main color (MC) and contrast color (CC) in this pattern. In most of my brioche patterns, the lighter color (LC) is the featured color, but when white is the background, it's easier to think in terms of MC and CC. Choose which of your colors you want to shine; that's your MC for this pattern. The ribbed ends are worked in the CC.

YARN

Worsted weight yarn in 2 contrasting colors | Shown in Knit Picks Chroma Worsted (70% Superwash Wool, 30% Nylon; 198 yards/181 meters in 100 g), 1 ball each color Pegasus (MC) and Bare (CC) | 119 yards/109 meters MC and 129 yards/118 meters CC for shorter cowl; one ball of each color is enough for either size

NEEDLES

US 6/4.0 mm 24"/60 cm circular needle for brioche, or size to attain gauge or a fabric you like

Needle one size larger for ribbing at beginning and end of cowl

GAUGE

16.5 sts in 4"/10 cm in two-color Brioche Rib worked flat, after steam blocking | Gauge not critical

NOTIONS

Tapestry needle
Six 7/8"/2.25 cm buttons
Needle and thread for attaching buttons

FINISHED SIZE

Brioche section is 6.5"/16.5 cm wide, 31 (52)"/79 (132) cm long for single (double) looped cowl

DIRECTIONS

BUTTON BAND

With CC and larger needle, CO 29 stitches using Long Tail Cast On.

Row 1 (WS): P4, *k3, p3; rep from * to last st, p1.
Row 2 (RS): K4, *p3, k3; rep from * to last st, k1.

Rep [Rows 1 & 2] 4 more times; 10 rows worked. Join MC; do not cut CC. Change to smaller needle.

Row 11 MC (WS): P2tog, *sl1yo, p1; rep from * to last 3 sts, sl1yo, p2tog. 2 sts dec, 27 sts rem. Slide work back to beginning of row.

Row 12 CC (WS): Sl1 wyif, yb, *brk, sl1yo; rep from * to last 2 sts, brk, yf, sl1 wyif. Turn work.

TWO-COLOR BRIOCHE

Each numbered row is worked first with MC, then with CC.

Row 1 MC (RS): K1, *sl1yo, brk; rep from * to last 2 sts, sl1yo, k1. Do not turn. Slide work back to beginning of row.

Row 1 CC (RS): Sl1 wyib, yf, *brp, sl1yo; rep from * to last 2 sts, brp, yb, sl1 wyib. Turn work.

Row 2 MC (WS): P1, *sl1yo, brp; rep from * to last 2 sts, sl1yo, p1. Slide.

Row 2 CC (WS): Sl1 wyif, yb, *brk, sl1yo; rep from * to last 2 sts, brk, yf, sl1 wyif. Turn.

Rep Rows 1 MC & CC and 2 MC & CC until brioche section measures 32 (52)"/ 79 (132) cm or desired length, ending with Row 2 CC. Cut MC, leaving 6"/15 cm tail.

BUTTONHOLE BAND

Setup Row (RS): K1, kfb, brk, *p1, brk; rep from * to last 2 sts, kfb, k1. 2 sts inc, 29 sts total. Change to larger needle.

Row 1 (WS): P4, *k3, p3; rep from * to last st, p1.

Row 2 (RS): K4, *p3, k3; rep from * to last st, k1.

Rows 3 & 4: Rep Rows 1 & 2.

Row 5: P1, (p2tog, yo, p1, k3, p3, k3) 2x, p2tog, yo, p2.

Rows 6 — 9: Work [Rows 2 & 3] 2 more times.

Row 10: Rep Row 2.

FINISHING

With WS facing, BO loosely in rib pattern. Sew in ends. Steam block. Sew buttons back-to-back on both RS and WS of button band, in line with the 3 buttonholes, so that cowl can be worn either side out. Cowl can be buttoned as a loop, or with ends overlapped and parallel. Best of all? Put a twist in it before buttoning for a colorful swirl!

Italian Soda Cowl with a twist (or two)

Peppermint Mocha Coaster

As I mentioned before, brioche can be so much more than just knit and purl ribbing. These eye-catching stockinette coasters have a secret! From the front, they look like vertical stockinette stripes, but if you peek at the back, you know it's brioche!

For matching cup cozy, see Peppermint Mocha Cup Cozy on page 28.

YARN
Worsted weight yarn in 2 contrasting colors | Shown in Malabrigo Rios (100% Superwash Wool, 210 yards/192 meters in 100 g), 1 skein each color English Rose (DC) and Almond Blossom (LC) | 10 yards/9 meters DC and 9 yards/8 meters LC for each coaster

NEEDLES
US 5/3.75 mm circular needle or set of 2 dpns for brioche, or size to attain gauge or a fabric you like

GAUGE
15 sts and 24 rows in 4"/10 cm in Stockinette Brioche worked flat, after steam blocking | Gauge not critical

NOTIONS
Tapestry needle

FINISHED SIZE
Coasters are approximately 4"/10 cm square

DIRECTIONS
With DC, loosely CO 17 sts using Long Tail Cast On. (Note: I leave space between stitches when casting on, so it's not tight.)

Setup Row DC (WS): P1, *sl1yo, p1; rep from * to end. Slide work back to beginning of row.

Setup Row LC (WS): Sl1 wyib, join LC, *brp, sl1yo; rep from * to last 2 sts, brp, yb, sl1 wyib. Turn work.

> **TIP** Where am I? If yarns are at opposite ends when you finish a row, the next move is to work the LC yarn to catch up with the DC.

TWO COLOR STOCKINETTE BRIOCHE
Each numbered row is worked first with DC, then with LC.

Row 1 DC (RS): K1, *sl1yo, brk; rep from * to last 2 sts, sl1yo, k1. Slide work back to beginning of row.

Row 1 LC (RS): Sl1 wyif, yb, *brk, sl1yo; rep from * to last 2 sts, brk, yf, sl1 wyif. Turn work.

Row 2 DC (WS): P1, *sl1yo, brp; rep from * to last 2 sts, sl1yo, p1. Slide.

Row 2 LC (WS): Sl1 wyib, yf, *brp, sl1yo; rep from * to last 2 sts, brp, yb, sl1 wyib. Turn.

Rep [Rows 1 DC & LC and 2 DC & LC] until piece measures 4"/10 cm, ending with Row 1 LC (RS). Cut LC, leaving 6"/15 cm tail.

FINISHING

With WS facing, BO purlwise with DC using Suspended Bind Off (see Special Techniques), working brp into the sl1yos and p the single stitches. Sew in ends. Steam block.

Peppermint Mocha Coaster right side

Peppermint Mocha Coaster wrong side

CHAPTER 5

Syncopated Brioche

In music, syncopation is a disturbance of the regular flow of rhythm, by playing on the off beat. In syncopated brioche, we're changing up the rhythm of our stitches. We'll exchange brioche knits for brioche purls, and vice versa for a stunning effect. In the Crema Cowl, we'll change the rhythm of entire rounds of knitting. In the Shortbread Scarf, we'll change the rhythm of the stitches within rows.

> **TIP** The secret to syncopation is to make sure that each sl1yo really does get its yo when you're switching from knits to purls, or purls to knits, at the point of syncopation.

ROW/ROUND NUMBERS

In the Crema Cowl, we're giving each round its own number. Odd numbered rounds are the MC, and even numbered rounds are the CC. Each round is actually only half a round; it takes two rounds to work all the stitches on your needle.

In the Shortbread Scarf, we're acknowledging that the LC and DC rounds are really half rounds, and naming them 1 LC & 1 DC, 2 LC & 2 DC, etc. This is conventional for brioche knitting. You'll see both ways of naming Row/Round numbers as you continue on your brioche journey.

READING CHARTS

In this chapter, I'm introducing you to brioche charts for the Shortbread Scarf. Reading a brioche chart is much like reading any other chart; the chart represents what the right side of your knitting looks like. Brioche charts look a little busier than normal because of all the brk, brp, and sl1yo symbols, but many brioche charts are mostly Brioche Rib. You need only pay attention to when things change, like an increase or decrease, or where the stitches syncopate.

Because each row or round requires two passes, you'll see the same number repeated for both the LC and DC, or MC and CC. If the numbers alternate between the left and right edges of the chart, the chart is meant to be knit flat, back and forth. You'll see the two passes that are needed before the numbers move to the other edge, telling you to turn your work. If all the numbers are on the right edge of the chart, the chart is meant to be knit in the round.

Instructions are given in both chart and written form.

Crema Cowl

The Crema Cowl is a sweet and simple introduction to the art of syncopated Brioche Rib. Using a gradient or ombre yarn will make the syncopated stripes even more interesting.

This cowl is knit from the bottom up, beginning with the CC rolled stockinette edging. There are three MC-dominant stripes, separated by two CC-dominant stripes in between. Another CC rolled stockinette edge completes the cowl. Choose the color you'd like to feature as your MC, so it has a chance to shine!

YARN

Worsted weight yarn in 2 contrasting colors | Shown in Knit Picks Chroma Worsted (70% Superwash Wool, 30% Nylon; 198 yards/181 meters in 100 g), 1 ball each color Drawing Room (MC) and Bare (CC) | 85 yards/78 meters MC and 120 yards/110 meters CC

NEEDLES

US 6/4.0 mm 24"/60 cm circular needle, or size to attain gauge or a fabric you like

GAUGE

16 sts and 24 rows in 4"/10 cm in Brioche Rib worked in the round, after steam blocking | Gauge not critical

NOTIONS

Tapestry needle
Stitch marker to denote beginning of round

FINISHED SIZE

24"/60 cm circumference, 7"/18 cm tall | If you prefer a taller cowl, increase the height of each of the 12-round syncopated sections in multiples of 2 rounds (i.e.: 14, 16, 18, etc). To adjust the circumference of the cowl, change cast on by a multiple of 2 sts.

DIRECTIONS

With CC, CO 96 sts using Long Tail Cast On. PM, join to work in the round. Knit 5 rounds.

Setup Rnd 1 (MC): Join MC. *K1, sl1yo; rep from * to end.
Setup Rnd 1 (CC): *Sl1yo, brp; rep from * to end.

SYNCOPATED BRIOCHE RIB

Rnd 1 (MC): *Brk, sl1yo; rep from * to end.

Rnd 2 (CC): *Sl1yo, brp; rep from * to end.

Rnds 3 – 12: Rep [Rnds 1 & 2] 5 more times.

Rnd 13 (MC): *Brp, sl1yo; rep from * to end. (Complete last yo, drop MC in front.)

Rnd 14 (CC): *Sl1yo, brk; rep from * to end. (Drop CC in back.)

Rnds 15 – 24: Rep [Rnds 13 & 14] 5 more times.

Rnds 25 – 48: Rep [Rnds 1 – 24] once more.

Rnds 49 – 60: Rep [Rnds 1 – 12] once more.

Rnds 61 – 62: Work [Rnds 1 – 2] once more, to balance the extra 2 setup rows from the beginning. Symmetry!

Brioche Closing Rnd (CC): *Brk, k1; rep from * to end. Cut MC, leaving 6"/15 cm tail.

With CC, knit 5 rnds.

FINISHING

BO all sts knitwise using Suspended Bind Off (see Special Techniques). Sew in ends. Steam block.

Crema Cowl

Shortbread Scarf

The alternating squares in the Shortbread Scarf are inspired by nine-patch quilt blocks. Their rhythmic pattern is perfect for syncopated brioche. Both sides of the scarf are lovely; choose which side to feature according to your mood.

In this pattern, I refer to the two colors as MC and CC. This is a small departure from many of my patterns (where I use LC and DC for color references), but when the background color is white, it's easier to think of your colors as MC and CC. When trying to decide, remember that the color you want to highlight most will be your MC.

YARN

Worsted weight yarn in 2 contrasting colors | Shown in Knit Picks Chroma Worsted (70% Superwash Wool, 30% Nylon; 198 yards/181 meters in 100 g), 1 ball each color Drawing Room (MC) and Bare (CC) | 198 yards/181 meters each MC and CC

NEEDLES

US 5/3.75 mm 24"/60 cm circular needle, or size to attain gauge or a fabric you like

GAUGE

15.5 sts and 24 rows in 4"/10 cm in Brioche Rib worked flat, before blocking | Gauge not critical

NOTIONS

Tapestry needle
4 stitch markers

FINISHED SIZE

8"/20 cm wide, 48"/122 cm long after light steam blocking

DIRECTIONS

Note for chart knitters: Place markers between sts 12 & 13, and 19 & 20 while working Row 9 MC. Slip markers on subsequent rows. Reset markers while working Row 17 MC: place markers between sts 6 & 7, 13 & 14, 18 & 19, and 25 & 26. Reset markers while working Row 25 MC, placing markers as you did for Row 9 MC. These markers indicate where to change/syncopate brioche stitches.

With MC, loosely CO 31 sts using Long Tail Cast On.

Setup Row 1 MC (WS): P1, *sl1yo, p1; rep from * to end. Slide work back to beginning of row.

Setup Row 2 CC (WS): Sl1 wyif, join CC from front, yb, brk, *sl1yo, brk; rep from * to last st, yf, sl1 wyif. Turn work.

Work Shortbread pattern from written instructions or chart. (See chart on next page)

Rows 1, 3, 5, 7 MC (RS): K1, sl1yo, (brk, sl1yo) 14x, k1. Do not turn. Slide work back to beginning of row.

Rows 1, 3, 5, 7 CC (RS): Sl1 wyib, yf, (brp, sl1yo) 14x, brp, yb, sl1 wyib. Turn work.

Rows 2, 4, 6, 8 MC (WS): P1, sl1yo, (brp, sl1yo) 14x, p1. Slide.

SHORTBREAD SCARF CHART

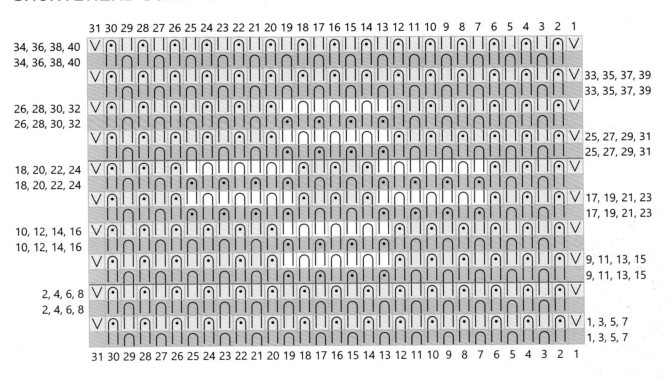

KEY

| | RS: knit / WS: purl | | RS: brk / WS: brp | | RS: brp / WS: brk |

☐ RS: knit
WS: purl

∩ RS: brk
WS: brp

⋒ RS: brp
WS: brk

|| sl1yo

V RS: slip purlwise wyib
WS: slip purlwise wyif

MC on MC dominant brioche

CC on MC dominant brioche

MC on CC dominant brioche

CC on CC dominant brioche

Repeat

Rows 2, 4, 6, 8 CC (WS): Sl1 wyif, yb, (brk, sl1yo) 14x, brk, yf, sl1 wyif. Turn.

Rows 9, 11, 13, 15 MC: K1, sl1yo, (brk, sl1yo) 5x, pm, brp, (sl1yo, brp) 3x, pm, (sl1yo, brk) 5x, sl1yo, k1. Slide. (Slip markers on subsequent rows after placing them on Row 9 MC.)

Rows 9, 11, 13, 15 CC: Sl1 wyib, yf, brp, (sl1yo, brp) 5x, sm, sl1yo, (brk, sl1yo) 3x, sm, brp, (sl1yo, brp) 5x, yb, sl1 wyib. Turn.

Rows 10, 12, 14, 16 MC: P1, sl1yo, (brp, sl1yo) 5x, sm, brk, (sl1yo, brk) 3x, sm, (sl1yo, brp) 5x, sl1yo, p1. Slide.

Rows 10, 12, 14, 16 CC: Sl1 wyif, yb, brk, (sl1yo, brk) 5x, sm, sl1yo, (brp, sl1yo) 3x, sm, brk, (sl1yo, brk) 5x, yf, sl1 wyif. Turn. Note: On Row 16 CC, remove markers as encountered.

Rows 17, 19, 21, 23 MC: K1, sl1yo, (brk, sl1yo) 2x, pm, brp, (sl1yo, brp) 3x, pm, sl1yo, (brk, sl1yo) 2x, pm, brp, (sl1yo, brp) 3x, pm, sl1yo, (brk, sl1yo) 2x, k1. Slide.

Rows 17, 19, 21, 23 CC: Sl1 wyib, yf, brp, (sl1yo, brp) 2x, sm, sl1yo, (brk, sl1yo) 3x, sm, brp, (sl1yo, brp) 2x, sm, sl1yo, (brk, sl1yo) 3x, sm, brp, (sl1yo, brp) 2x, yb, sl1 wyib. Turn.

Rows 18, 20, 22, 24 MC: P1, sl1yo, (brp, sl1yo) 2x, sm, brk, (sl1yo, brk) 3x, sm, sl1yo, (brp, sl1yo) 2x, sm, brk, (sl1yo, brk) 3x, sm, sl1yo, (brp, sl1yo) 2x, p1. Slide.

Rows 18, 20, 22, 24 CC: Sl1 wyif, yb, brk, (sl1yo, brk) 2x, sm, sl1yo, (brp, sl1yo) 3x, sm, brk, (sl1yo, brk) 2x, sm, sl1yo, (brp, sl1yo) 3x, sm, brk, (sl1yo, brk) 2x, yf, sl1 wyif. Turn. Note: On Row 24 CC, remove markers as encountered.

Rep [Rows 9 MC & CC – 24 MC & CC] 14 more times or until the scarf is 3"/7.5 cm shorter than desired length, ending with Row 24 CC. Then work finishing [Rows 25 MC & CC – 40 MC & CC] once.

Rows 25, 27, 29, 31 MC: Work same as Rows 9, 11, 13, 15 MC.

Rows 25, 27, 29, 31 CC: Work same as Rows 9, 11, 13, 15 CC.

Rows 26, 28, 30, 32 MC: Work same as Rows 10, 12, 14, 16 MC.

Rows 26, 28, 30, 32 CC: Work same as Rows 10, 12, 14, 16 CC.

Rows 33, 35, 37, 39 MC: Work same as Rows 1, 3, 5, 7 MC.

Rows 33, 35, 37, 39 CC: Work same as Rows 1, 3, 5, 7 CC.

Rows 34, 36, 38, 40 MC: Work same as Rows 2, 4, 6, 8 MC.

Rows 34, 36, 38, 40 CC: Work same as Rows 2, 4, 6, 8 CC. Cut CC, leaving 6"/15 cm tail.

Closing Row MC (RS): K1, *p1, brk; rep from * to last 2 sts, p1, k1.

FINISHING
With WS facing, BO loosely in ribbing pattern. Sew in ends. Gently steam block.

CHOCOLATE CHIP SHORTBREAD RECIPE

Bonus! Here's some real shortbread to go with your latte. This recipe is a family favorite.

INGREDIENTS

1/2 cup butter, softened
1/2 cup sugar
1 teaspoon vanilla
1 and 1/4 cup flour
1/4 teaspoon salt
1/2 cup miniature semisweet chocolate chips

DIRECTIONS

Preheat oven to 375 degrees.

Beat butter and sugar with electric mixer until light and fluffy. Beat in vanilla. Combine flour and salt, then beat together with the butter/sugar mixture. (It will be crumbly.) Stir in chips. Press into an ungreased 9 inch square pan.

Bake 18-20 minutes or until edges are golden. Cool 15 minutes in pan on wire rack.

Score shortbread with sharp knife into desired size servings, but do not cut all the way through. Invert onto rack and cool completely. Break into squares.

Chocolate Chip Shortbread

CHAPTER 6

Brioche Increases and Decreases

Brioche increases and decreases break us out of our columns of Brioche Rib, and allow the columns to meander into flowing motifs. Increases and decreases are usually made in multiples of 2 stitches to keep the brioche rhythm. Patterns in this book will always increase or decrease by 2 or 4 stitches at a time. Paired yarn overs are considered part of their associated stitches; so knit or slip or pass them along with their stitches. Ready to explore?

See Resources on page 121 for additional assistance.

brkyobrk, brioche 2 stitch increase

Brioche knit, but leave st on left needle.

Yarn over.

Brioche knit, all in the same stitch. 2 stitches increased.

Completed brkyobrk. When working the next row or round, work a plain purl or plain knit stitch in the center stitch of the increase (it doesn't have a paired yarn over yet), whichever is appropriate in the row/round you're working.

br4st inc, brioche 4 stitch increase

Brioche knit, yarn over, brioche knit, yarn over, brioche knit, all in the same stitch. 4 stitches increased.

Completed br4st inc.

brdecL, brioche left leaning double decrease

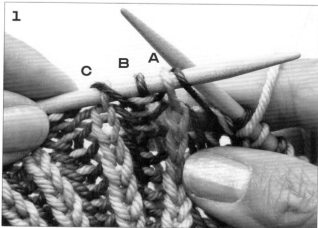

Worked over 3 stitches.

brdecL (continued from last page)

Slip A knitwise.

Knit B and C together.

Pass A over and off. 2 stitches decreased.

Completed brdecL.

brdecR, Right leaning double decrease

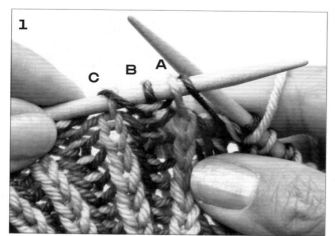

Worked over 3 stitches.

Slip A knitwise, slip B knitwise, separately.

Insert left needle into fronts of these 2 stitches and knit them off together through back loops.

Move resulting stitch to left needle.

Pass C over and off left needle.

Move finished stitch to right needle and snug up.
2 stitches decreased.

Completed brdecR.

bruwdec, brioche unwrapped double decrease, an alternate for brdecL

This decrease hides the shadow of the wrap of the passed over stitch. Tidy! It can be used in place of brdecL. (This stitch was developed by Xandy Peters.)

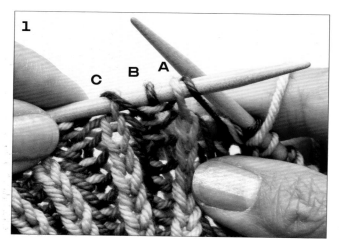

Worked over 3 stitches.

Slip A knitwise, slip B knitwise, separately.

Move yo from A, and stitch B, back to left needle, working left needle tip from right to left.

Knit C, yo from A, and B all together. (knitting through 4 strands of yarn from left needle)

Pass unwrapped A over and off. 2 stitches decreased.

Completed unwrapped left leaning decrease.

br4st dec, brioche 4 stitch decrease

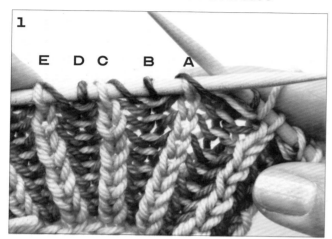

Worked over 5 stitches.

Slip A knitwise, slip B knitwise, separately.

Place C on a removable stitch marker or cable hook, hanging in front of work.

Knit D.

...continued on next page

Pass B over D.

Slip D back to left needle, then pass E over D.

Slip D back to right needle, then pass A over D.

Place C back on left needle.

...continued on next page

Slip D to left needle, then pass C over D.

Move completed stitch to right needle, and snug it up. Completed br4st dec.

MORE ON READING CHARTS

Increases and decreases don't always line up on the chart the way they do in your knitting. And sometimes there's the mysterious "no stitch." Fear not, just move on to the next chart symbol and keep knitting. You don't have to use charts; I always give instructions in both chart and written form. I find them easier to follow than trying to keep my place in a line of text, but as long as you get the result you want, you're doing it right!

TIP Confused about reading charts, or confused about the number of rows/rounds to repeat in the written instructions? Check the chart against the written instructions, or the written instructions against the chart for clarity.

Photo at right: Coffee Breakers Cowl. See page 107 for pattern.

Iced Latte Hat

I loved the Iced Latte Cowl (page 30) so much I wanted to design a coordinating hat to go with it. The checkerboard brim folds up to create a double layer over your ears for extra warmth. You can show more or less of the brim. It's up to you. Your light color is featured on the brim, and the dark color is featured on the body of the hat. If you sew your ends in carefully, it's fully reversible, and you can feature your dark color on the brim, and the light color on the body of the hat, just by turning it inside out.

The Iced Latte Hat is worked in the round from the bottom up. Because of the large pattern repeat, the finished size can only be adjusted by changing your needle size or weight of yarn. Due to the magic stretchiness of brioche, you can adjust the fit of the hat for a larger head (without changing the needle size or weight of yarn) just by making the hat a little taller. Stretching it wider will steal a bit from the height.

This pattern introduces just one new stitch, brdecR, the brioche right leaning double decrease. It doesn't happen until the crown shaping, so you can cruise along until it's time to learn something new.

YARN

DK weight yarn in 2 contrasting colors | Shown in Hazel Knits Lively DK (90% Superwash Merino, 10% nylon, 275 yards/252 meters in 130 g), 1 skein each color Iris (DC) and Cackle (LC) | 135 yards/123 meters DC and 95 yards/87 meters LC

NEEDLES

US 5/3.75 mm 16"/40 cm circular needle, or size to attain gauge | same size dpns or extra circular or long circular for magic loop, to close top of hat

GAUGE

19 sts in 4"/10 cm in Brioche Rib worked in the round, after light steam blocking

NOTIONS

Tapestry needle
Stitch markers (7)

FINISHED SIZE

17.5"/44.5 cm circumference, 8"/20 cm tall with brim folded

DIRECTIONS

With DC, loosely CO 84 sts using Long Tail Cast On. PM, join to work in the round. Knit 1 round.

Work Iced Latte from chart or written instructions. (See chart on next page.)

Setup Rnd 1 (DC): *K6, (k1, sl1yo) 3x, pm; rep from * to end (a final marker will not be placed at the end of round as the BOR marker is already in place). After last sl1yo, leave DC in front. All DC brim rnds end with yarn in front.

Setup Rnd 2 (LC): *K6, (sl1yo, brk) 3x; rep from * to end. Leave LC yarn in back. All LC brim rnds end with yarn in back.

ICED LATTE BRIM

Worked over 12 sts and 24 rounds.

Rnds 1, 3, 5, 7, 9 (DC): *P6, (brp, sl1yo) 3x; rep from * to end.

Rnds 2, 4, 6, 8, 10 (LC): *K6, (sl1yo, brk) 3x; rep from * to end.

ICED LATTE STITCH CHART

12 11 10 9 8 7 6 5 4 3 2 1	
	24
	23
	14, 16, 18, 20, 22
	13, 15, 17, 19, 21
	12
	11
	2, 4, 6, 8, 10
	1, 3, 5, 7, 9
	Setup Rnd 2
	Setup Rnd 1

12 11 10 9 8 7 6 5 4 3 2 1

KEY

- ☐ knit
- • purl
- ∩ brk
- ⌐•⌐ brp
- || sl1yo
- ☐ Setup rnds
- ☐ Pattern Repeat
- ▨ DC rnds
- ☐ LC rnds

Rnd 11 (DC): *(P1, sl1yo)3x, (brp, p1) 3x; rep from * to end.

Rnd 12 (LC): *(Sl1yo, brk) 3x, k6; rep from * to end.

Rnds 13, 15, 17, 19, 21 (DC): *(brp, sl1yo) 3x, p6; rep from * to end.

Rnds 14, 16, 18, 20, 22 (LC): *(Sl1yo, brk) 3x, k6; rep from * to end.

Rnd 23 (DC): *(Brp, p1) 3x, (p1, sl1yo) 3x; rep from * to end.

Rnd 24 (LC): *K6, (sl1yo, brk) 3x; rep from * to end.

Rep Rnds 1 – 24 of Iced Latte Stitch pattern once, then work Rnds 1 – 10 once more.

Transition Rnd (DC): *(p1, sl1yo) 3x, (brp, sl1yo) 3x; rep from * to end. Remove BOR m, p1, replace BOR m. Beginning of rnd shifts one st to the left.

BRIOCHE RIB HAT BODY

Body is knit in LC Brioche Rib, but it will be the inside of the hat when the brim is folded up. LC brk sts will continue in the same columns above Iced Latte brim. The transition will be at the fold line between brim and hat body.

Rnd 1 (LC): *Brk, sl1yo; rep from * to end.

Rnd 2 (DC): *Sl1yo, brp; rep from * to end.

Rep Rnds 1 and 2 until hat body measures 7"/18 cm from the Transition Rnd.

CROWN

Rnd 1 (LC): *(Brk, sl1yo) 5x, brdecR, sl1yo; rep from * to end. 72 sts.

Rnds 2 – 4: Work Rnds 2, 1 & 2 of Brioche Rib Hat Body as shown above.

Rnd 5 (LC): *(Brk, sl1yo) 4x, brdecR, sl1yo; rep from * to end. 60 sts.

Rnds 6 – 8: Work Rnds 2, 1 & 2 of Brioche Rib Hat Body.

Rnd 9 (LC): *(Brk, sl1yo) 3x, brdecR, sl1yo; rep from * to end. 48 sts.

Rnds 10 – 12: Work Rnds 2, 1 & 2 of Brioche Rib Hat Body.

Rnd 13 (LC): *(Brk, sl1yo) 2x, brdecR, sl1yo; rep from * to end. 36 sts.

Rnds 14 – 16: Work Rnds 2, 1 & 2 of Brioche Rib Hat Body.

Rnd 17 (LC): *Brk, sl1yo, brdecR, sl1yo; rep from * to end. 24 sts.

Rnds 18 – 20: Work Rnds 2, 1 & 2 of Brioche Rib Hat Body.

Rnd 21 (LC): *BrdecR, sl1yo; rep from * to end. 12 sts.

Rnd 22 (DC): *K1, brk; rep from * to end.

FINISHING

Cut both yarns, leaving 8"/20 cm tail. Use tapestry needle to run DC through remaining sts twice, and cinch tightly. Sew in ends on LC side of hat. Lightly steam block. Fold up brim.

You can decide how deep to fold your brim, with more or less Iced Latte showing. If you are careful sewing in your ends, you can make this hat completely reversible.

Iced Latte Hat with folded brim

Berry Galette Cowl

Twenty years ago, we planted blueberry bushes in our garden. One of them is particularly happy; we get gallons of berries every summer. The leaves and bumps of the Berry Galette Cowl reminds me of that cheerful bush and makes me dream of blueberry desserts.

The Berry Galette Cowl is knit in the round from the bottom up. Increases and decreases form the leafy pattern. The berries are also created with increases and decreases, but the berry increase isn't decreased away until a couple of rounds later. Your stitch count will increase and decrease periodically during these rounds, but all will be well!

YARN

Worsted weight yarn in 2 contrasting colors | Shown in Malabrigo Rios (100% Superwash Wool, 210 yards/192 meters in 100 g), 1 skein each color Azules (DC) and Aquamarine (LC) | 126 yards/115 meters DC and 90 yards/82 meters LC

NEEDLES

US 6/4.0 mm 16 or 24"/40 or 60 cm circular needle, or size to attain gauge or a fabric you like

GAUGE

18 sts in 4"/10 cm in Berry Galette pattern worked in the round, after blocking | Gauge not critical

NOTIONS

Tapestry needle
Stitch markers (12)

FINISHED SIZE

21"/53 cm circumference, 7"/18 cm tall, size adjustable

DIRECTIONS

With DC, CO 96 sts using Long Tail Cast On. PM (unique marker for BOR), join to work in the rounds. Knit 6 rounds.

Work Berry Galette pattern from written instructions or chart. **For chart knitters:** note that markers should be placed on Rnd 1 LC after each chart repeat. (See chart on next page.)

BERRY GALETTE PATTERN

Setup Rnd LC: *K1, sl1yo; rep from * to end.
Setup Rnd DC: *Sl1yo, brp; rep from * to end.

Rnd 1 LC: *Brkyobrk, sl1yo, brdecL, sl1yo, brkyobrk, sl1yo, pm; rep from * to end (a final marker will not be placed at the end of round as the BOR marker is already in place). 120 sts. (On subsequent Rnd 1 LC, sm as you come to them.)

Rnd 1 DC: *Sl1yo, p1, (sl1yo, brp) 2x, sl1yo, p1, sl1yo, brp, sm; rep from * to end.

Rnd 2 LC: *Brk, sl1yo; rep from * to end.

Rnd 2 DC: *Sl1yo, brp; rep from * to end.

Rnd 3 LC: *Brkyobrk, sl1yo, brdecL, sl1yo, brdecR, sl1yo, sm; rep from * to end. 96 sts.

BERRY GALETTE COWL CHART

KEY

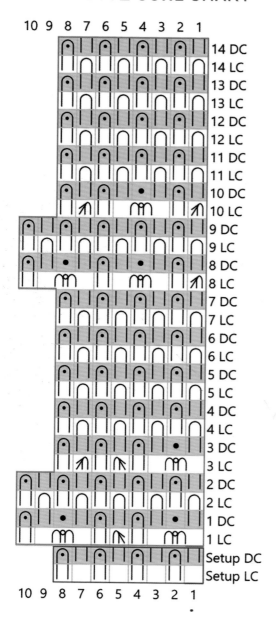

☐	RS: knit
•	purl
⋒	RS: brk
⋒	RS: brp
‖	sl1yo
⋒	brkyobrk
⋔	brdecL
⋔	brdecR
☐	Berry Galette repeat
☐	Setup Rnds
☐	LC
▨	DC

Rnd 3 DC: *Sl1yo, p1, (sl1yo, brp) 3x, sm; rep from * to end.

Rnds 4 LC & DC – 7 LC & DC: Rep [Rnds 2 LC & DC] 4 times.

Rnd 8 LC: *BrdecR, (sl1yo, brkyobrk) 2x, sl1yo, sm; rep from * to end. 120 sts

Rnd 8 DC: *(Sl1yo, brp, sl1yo, p1) 2x, sl1yo, brp, sm; rep from * to end.

Rnds 9 LC & DC: Repeat Rnds 2 LC & DC.

Rnd 10 LC: *BrdecR, sl1yo, brkyobrk, sl1yo, brdecR, sl1yo, sm; rep from * to end. 96 sts.

Rnd 10 DC: *Sl1yo, brp, sl1yo, p1, (sl1yo, brp) 2x, sm; rep from * to end.

Rnds 11 LC & DC – 14 LC & DC: Rep [Rnds 2 LC & DC] 4 times.

Rep [Rnds 1 LC & DC – 14 LC & DC] to desired height, ending with Rnd 7 DC or 14 DC. Cut LC, leaving 6"/15 cm tail.

If you ended with Rnd 7 DC:

Rnd 1 (DC, not LC): *BrdecR, sl1yo, brkyobrk, sl1yo, brk, sl1yo, sm; rep from *to end.

Rnd 2: *K1, brp, k3, brp, k1, brp, remove marker; rep from * to end (leaving BOR marker in place).

If you ended with Rnd 14 DC:

Rnd 1 (DC, not LC): *Brkyobrk, sl1yo, brdecL, sl1yo, brk, sl1yo, sm; rep to end.

Rnd 2: *K3, (brp, k1) 2x, brp, remove marker; rep from * to end (leaving BOR marker in place).

Knit 5 rnds with DC.

FINISHING

BO all sts knitwise using Suspended Bind Off (see Special Techniques). Sew in ends. Steam or wet block.

Berry Galette Cowl

Berry Galette Wristlets

Wrist warmers are the perfect defense against a chilly breeze up your sleeve! These wristlets are a great project to use up any leftover yarn from your Berry Galette Cowl.

The Berry Galette Wristlets are knit in the round from the bottom up. They're knit on a smaller needle than the cowl to create a slightly denser gauge. The Berry Galette stitch pattern is featured just once on the front of the wristlet, while the rest of the wristlet is plain Brioche Rib. If you'd like to adjust the size, increase or decrease your cast on by a multiple of 2 stitches, to be worked in the plain Brioche Rib section.

YARN

Worsted weight yarn in 2 contrasting colors | Shown in Malabrigo Rios (100% Superwash Wool, 210 yards/192 meters in 100 g), 1 skein each color Azules (DC) and Aquamarine (LC) | 50 yards/46 meters DC and 40 yards/37 meters LC

NEEDLES

US 4/3.5 mm set of 4 or 5 dpns or 2 circular needles or one 32"/80 cm circular for magic loop to work small circumference, or size to attain gauge

GAUGE

18 sts in 4"/10 cm in Brioche Rib worked in the round, after blocking

NOTIONS

Tapestry needle
Stitch markers (2)

FINISHED SIZE

Small (Medium, Large)

7 (8, 9)"/18 (20.5, 23) cm circumference, 5"/12.5 cm tall, size adjustable

DIRECTIONS

With DC, loosely CO 28 (32, 36) sts using Long Tail Cast On. PM, join to work in the round. Knit 1 round.

Join LC (don't cut DC). Knit 1 rnd. Purl 1 rnd.

Change to DC, knit 1 rnd. Bring DC to front of work.

Work Berry Galette Wristlets from written instructions or chart. **For chart knitters:** place a marker on each side of the Berry Galette panel on Rnd 1; sm on all subsequent rnds. (See chart on next page.)

Setup Rnd LC: *K1, sl1yo; rep from * to end.

> **TIP** At end of the round, drop LC at front of work without creating the final yo; it will hang between last 2 sts of rnd. All LC rnds end this way. Last st of rnd is missing its yo; it will get its yo at end of next rnd. (This is the "delayed" gratification method of handling your beginning/end of round as described on page 26.)

Setup Rnd DC: *Sl1yo, brp; rep from * to end.

BERRY GALETTE WRISTLETS CHART

KEY

□	knit
•	purl
∩	brk
⨀	brp
‖	sl1yo
⋏	brdecL
⋌	brdecR
ᙏ	brkyobrk
□	Setup Rnds
□	Berry Galette panel
□	Brioche Rib repeat
✕	no stitch
▨	DC
□	LC

Chart columns: 18 17 16 15 14 13 12 11 10 9 8 7 6 5 4 3 2 1

Chart rows: 14 DC, 14 LC, 13 DC, 13 LC, 12 DC, 12 LC, 11 DC, 11 LC, 10 DC, 10 LC, 9 DC, 9 LC, 8 DC, 8 LC, 7 DC, 7 LC, 6 DC, 6 LC, 5 DC, 5 LC, 4 DC, 4 LC, 3 DC, 3 LC, 2 DC, 2 LC, 1 DC, 1 LC, Setup DC, Setup LC

Rnd 1 LC: Brk, sl1yo, pm, (brkyobrk, sl1yo) 2x, brdecL, sl1yo, brkyobrk, sl1yo, pm, *brk, sl1yo; rep from * to end. 32 (36, 40) sts. (On subsequent repeat of Rnd 1 LC, sm as you come to them.)

Rnd 1 DC: Sl1yo, brp, sm, (sl1yo, p1, sl1yo, brp) 2x, sl1yo, brp, sl1yo, p1, sl1yo, brp, sm, * sl1yo, brp; rep from * to end.

Rnd 2 LC: *Brk, sl1yo; rep from * to end.

Rnd 2 DC: *Sl1yo, brp; rep from * to end.

Rnd 3 LC: Brk, sl1yo, sm, brdecR, sl1yo, brkyobrk, sl1yo, brdecL, sl1yo, brdecR, sl1yo, sm, *brk, sl1yo; rep from * to end. 28 (32, 36) sts.

Rnd 3 DC: Sl1yo, brp, sm, sl1yo, brp, sl1yo, p1, (sl1yo, brp) 3x, sm, *sl1yo, brp; rep from * to end.

Rnds 4 LC & DC – 7 LC & DC: Rep [Rnds 2 LC & DC] 4 times.

Rnd 8 LC: Brk, sl1yo, sm, brkyobrk, sl1yo, brdecR, sl1yo, (brkyobrk, sl1yo) 2x, sm, *brk, sl1yo; rep from * to end. 32 (36, 40) sts.

Rnd 8 DC: Sl1yo, brp, sm, sl1yo, p1, (sl1yo, brp) 2x, (sl1yo, p1, sl1yo, brp) 2x, sm, *sl1yo, brp; rep from * to end.

Rnds 9 LC & DC: Rep Rnds 2 LC & DC.

Rnd 10 LC: Brk, sl1yo, sm, (brdecR, sl1yo) 2x, brkyobrk, sl1yo, brdecR, sl1yo, *brk, sl1yo; rep from * to end. 28 (32, 36) sts.

Rnd 10 DC: Sl1yo, brp, sm, (sl1yo, brp) 2x, sl1yo, p1, (sl1yo, brp) 2x, sm, *sl1yo, brp; rep from * to end.

Rnds 11 LC & DC – 14 LC & DC: Rep [Rnds 2 LC & DC] 4 times.

Rep [Rnds 1 LC & DC – 10 LC & DC] once more.

Closing Rnd (DC): *Brk, k1; rep from * to end.

With LC, knit 1 rnd. Purl 1 rnd. Cut LC, leaving 6"/15 cm tail.

With DC, knit 1 rnd.

FINISHING
BO all stitches loosely knitwise using Suspended Bind Off (see Special Techniques). Sew in ends. Steam or wet block.

Berry Galette Wristlets

Green Tea Chai Scarf

Mmmmmm, green tea. Mellower than coffee, but every bit as delightful. Relax into your knitting with the the repeating tea leaf motif of this scarf.

The Green Tea Chai Scarf adds one more increase to your brioche toolbox, br4st inc, the brioche 4 stitch increase. You can also think of it as brkyobrkyobrk; it's like the brkyobrk with a little extra pizzazz! The Green Tea Chai stitch pattern is easy to memorize, and it's a great opportunity to learn to read your knitting.

YARN
Worsted weight yarn in 2 contrasting colors | Shown in Malabrigo Rios (100% Superwash Wool, 210 yards/192 meters in 100 g), 1 skein each color Solis (DC) and Water Green (LC) | 140 yards/128 meters DC and 175 yards/160 meters LC

NEEDLES
US 6/4.0 mm 24"/60 cm circular needle, or size to attain gauge or a fabric you like

GAUGE
23 sts in 4"/10 cm in Brioche Rib worked flat, after blocking | Gauge not critical

NOTIONS
Tapestry needle

FINISHED SIZE
5"/13 cm wide, 58"/147 cm long after wet blocking (this grew quite a bit in length)

DIRECTIONS
With LC, CO 29 sts using Long Tail Cast On. Work Green Tea Chai Scarf from written instructions or chart. (See next page for chart.)

GREEN TEA CHAI SCARF
Setup Row LC (WS): (P1, sl1yo) 14x, p1. Slide work back to beginning of row.

Setup Row DC (WS): Sl1 wyif, yb, (brk, sl1yo) 13x, brk, yf, sl1 wyif. Turn work.

Row 1 LC (RS): K1, (sl1yo, brk) 4x, sl1yo, brdecR, sl1yo, br4st inc, sl1yo, brdecL, (sl1yo, brk) 4x, sl1yo, k1. Slide.

Row 1 DC (RS): Sl1 wyib, yf, (brp, sl1yo) 6x, p1, sl1yo, p1, (sl1yo, brp) 6x, yb, sl1 wyib. Turn.

Row 2 LC: P1, (sl1yo, brp) 13x, sl1yo, p1. Slide.

Row 2 DC: Sl1 wyif, yb, (brk, sl1yo) 13x, brk, yf, sl1 wyif. Turn.

Row 3 LC: K1, (sl1yo, brk) 3x, sl1yo, brdecR, sl1yo, brkyobrk, sl1yo, brk, sl1yo, brkyobrk, sl1yo, brdecL, (sl1yo, brk) 3x, sl1yo, k1. Slide.

GREEN TEA CHAI SCARF

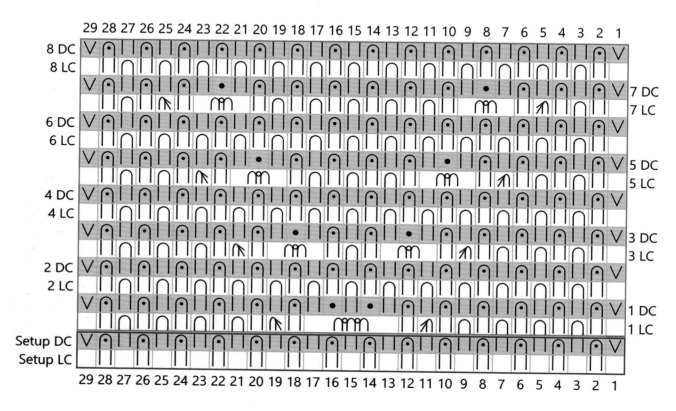

KEY

	RS: knit / WS: purl
	RS: purl / WS: knit
	RS: sl1 wyib / WS: sl1 wyif
	RS: brk / WS: brp

	RS: brp / WS: brk
	sl1yo
	RS: brdecR
	RS: brdecL

	br4st inc
	brkyobrk
	Green Tea Chai repeat
	Setup Rows

| | DC Row |
| | LC Row |

Row 3 DC: Sl1 wyib, yf, (brp, sl1yo) 2x, brp, [(sl1yo, brp) 2x, sl1yo, p1] 2x, (sl1yo, brp) 5x, yb, sl1 wyib. Turn.

Rows 4 LC & DC: Rep Rows 2 LC & DC.

Row 5 LC: K1, (sl1yo, brk) 2x, sl1yo, brdecR, sl1yo, brkyobrk, (sl1yo, brk) 3x, sl1yo, brkyobrk, sl1yo, brdecL, (sl1yo, brk) 2x, sl1yo, k1. Slide.

Row 5 DC: Sl1 wyib, yf, [(brp, sl1yo) 4x, p1, sl1yo] 2x, (brp, sl1yo) 3x, brp, yb, sl1 wyib. Turn.

Rows 6 LC & DC: Rep Rows 2 LC & DC.

Row 7 LC: K1, sl1yo, brk, sl1yo, brdecR, sl1yo, brkyobrk, (sl1yo, brk) 5x, sl1yo, brkyobrk, sl1yo, brdecL, sl1yo, brk, sl1yo, k1. Slide.

Row 7 DC: Sl1 wyib, yf, (brp, sl1yo) 3x, p1, (sl1yo, brp) 6x, sl1yo, p1, (sl1yo, brp) 3x, yb, sl1 wyib. Turn.

Rows 8 LC & DC: Rep Rows 2 LC & DC.

Rep [Rows 1 LC & DC – 8 LC & DC] 29 times, or to desired length, ending with Row 8 DC. Then work Rows 1 LC & DC – 4 LC & DC once more. Cut DC, leaving 6"/15 cm tail.

FINISHING

Using LC, BO loosely in ribbing pattern using Suspended Bind Off (see Special Techniques), working brk into the sl1yos and p the single purl stitches. Sew in ends. Steam or wet block.

Green Tea Chai Scarf

Latte Leaf Coaster and Cup Cozy

Have you ever noticed the pretty leaves that baristas make to decorate lattes? This coaster and cup cozy set celebrates the humble leaf, while giving you a chance to play with both flat (coaster) and circular (cozy) knitting. They feature a lighter color (LC) syncopated brioche leaf on a darker color (DC) Brioche Rib background. The leaf is a bit taller on the coaster, and shorter on the cup cozy. This is intentional. (Yes, technically, these patterns are extra credit knitting because they combine syncopation, as well as increases and decreases, but the latte leaves go so well with our current coffee and pastry theme. Let's roll with it!)

I've said that gauge is not critical for most of the projects in this book, but you'll want to make sure your cup cozy isn't too loose for your cup. No sliding cups of hot coffee! You can either adjust your cozy by needle size, or by changing the cast on by a multiple of 2 stitches to adjust the ribbing section that follows the leaf.

> **TIP** Use the Brioche Unwrapped Decrease (bruwdec) in place of the brioche left leaning double decrease (brdecL) in both Latte Leaf patterns for really crisp lines. The right and left leaning decreases will mirror each other perfectly.

YARN

Worsted weight yarn in 2 contrasting colors | Shown in Malabrigo Rios (100% Superwash Wool, 210 yards/192 meters in 100 g), 1 skein each color Aguas (DC) and Water Green (LC) | 13 yards/12 meters of each color for one coaster | 21 yards/19 meters (DC) and 16 yards/15 meters (LC) for one cup cozy

NEEDLES

Coaster: US 5/3.75 mm circular or double pointed needles, or size to attain gauge or a fabric you like

Cup Cozy: US 5/3.75 mm set of 4 or 5 dpns or 2 circular needles or one 32"/80 cm circular for magic loop to work small circumference, or size to attain gauge

GAUGE

17 sts in 4"/10 cm in Latte Leaf pattern worked flat and/or in the round, wet blocked

NOTIONS

Tapestry needle
Stitch marker to denote beginning of round on cup cozy (optional, depending on where you put your beginning of round)

FINISHED SIZE

Coaster: Approximately 4.5"/11 cm square

Cup Cozy: 8.5"/21.5 cm circumference, 3.5"/9 cm tall

Latte Leaf Coasters

LATTE LEAF COASTER CHART

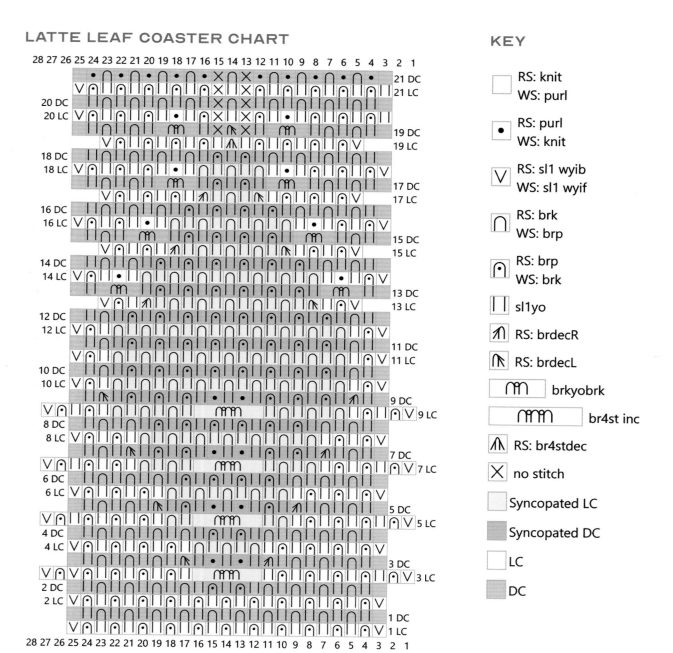

KEY

☐	RS: knit / WS: purl
•	RS: purl / WS: knit
V	RS: sl1 wyib / WS: sl1 wyif
∩	RS: brk / WS: brp
⋒	RS: brp / WS: brk
‖	sl1yo
⟍	RS: brdecR
⟋	RS: brdecL
⋔⋔	brkyobrk
⋔⋔⋔	br4st inc
⋀	RS: br4stdec
X	no stitch
(light)	Syncopated LC
(dark)	Syncopated DC
(white)	LC
(gray)	DC

DIRECTIONS: LATTE LEAF COASTER

With DC, loosely CO 23 sts using Long Tail Cast On.

Setup Row DC (WS): P1, *sl1yo, p1; rep from * to end. Turn work.

Work Latte Leaf Coaster pattern from written instructions or chart. (See chart at left.)

Row 1 LC (RS): Join LC. Sl1 wyib, yf, (brp, sl1yo) 10x, brp, yb, sl1 wyib. Slide.

Row 1 DC (RS): K1, (sl1yo, brk) 10x, sl1yo, k1. Turn.

Row 2 LC (WS): Sl1 wyif, yb, (brk, sl1yo) 10x, brk, yf, sl1 wyif. Slide.

Row 2 DC (WS): P1, (sl1yo, brp) 4x, (sl1yo, brk) 2x, (sl1yo, brp) 4x, sl1yo, p1. Turn.

Row 3 LC: Sl1 wyib, yf, (brp, sl1yo) 5x, br4st inc, (sl1yo, brp) 5x, yb, sl1 wyib. 27 sts. Slide.

Row 3 DC: K1, (sl1yo, brk) 3x, sl1yo, brdecR, (sl1yo, p1) 2x, sl1yo, brdecL, (sl1yo, brk) 3x, sl1yo, k1. 23 sts. Turn.

Row 4 LC: Sl1 wyif, yb, (brk, sl1yo) 4x, (brp, sl1yo) 2x, brp, (sl1yo, brk) 4x, yf, sl1 wyif. Slide.

Row 4 DC: Rep Row 2 DC.

Row 5 LC: Sl1 wyib, yf, (brp, sl1yo) 4x, brk, sl1yo, br4st inc, sl1yo, brk, (sl1yo, brp) 4x, yb, sl1 wyib. 27 sts. Slide.

Row 5 DC: K1, (sl1yo, brk) 2x, sl1yo, brdecR, sl1yo, brp, (sl1yo, p1) 2x, sl1yo, brp, sl1yo, brdecL, (sl1yo, brk) 2x, sl1yo, k1. 23 sts. Turn.

Row 6 LC: Sl1 wyif, yb, (brk, sl1yo) 2x, brk, (sl1yo, brp) 5x, (sl1yo, brk) 3x, yf, sl1 wyif. Slide.

Row 6 DC: P1, (sl1yo, brp) 3x, (sl1yo, brk) 4x, (sl1yo, brp) 3x, sl1yo, p1. Turn.

Row 7 LC: Sl1 wyib, yf, (brp, sl1yo) 3x, (brk, sl1yo) 2x, br4st inc, (sl1yo, brk) 2x, (sl1yo, brp) 3x, yb, sl1 wyib. 27 sts. Slide.

Row 7 DC: K1, sl1yo, brk, sl1yo, brdecR, (sl1yo, brp) 2x, (sl1yo, p1) 2x, (sl1yo, brp) 2x, sl1yo, brdecL, sl1yo, brk, sl1yo, k1. 23 sts. Turn.

Row 8 LC: Sl1 wyif, yb, brk, sl1yo, brk, (sl1yo, brp) 7x, (sl1yo, brk) 2x, yf, sl1 wyif. Slide.

Row 8 DC: P1, (sl1yo, brp) 2x, (sl1yo, brk) 6x, (sl1yo, brp) 2x, sl1yo, p1. Turn.

Row 9 LC: Sl1 wyib, yf, brp, sl1yo, brp, (sl1yo, brk) 3x, sl1yo, br4st inc, (sl1yo, brk) 3x, (sl1yo, brp) 2x, yb, sl1 wyib. 27 sts. Slide.

Row 9 DC: K1, sl1yo, brdecR, (sl1yo, brp) 3x, (sl1yo, p1) 2x, (sl1yo, brp) 3x, sl1yo, brdecL, sl1yo, k1. 23 sts. Turn.

Row 10 LC: Sl1 wyif, yb, brk, (sl1yo, brp) 9x, sl1yo, brk, yf, sl1 wyif. Slide.

Row 10 DC: P1, sl1yo, brp, (sl1yo, brk) 8x, sl1yo, brp, sl1yo, p1. Turn.

Row 11 LC: Sl1 wyib, yf, brp, (sl1yo, brk) 9x, sl1yo, brp, yb, sl1 wyib. Slide.

Row 11 DC: K1, sl1yo, brk, (sl1yo, brp) 8x, sl1yo, brk, sl1yo, k1. Turn.

Rows 12 LC & DC: Rep Rows 10 LC & DC.

Row 13 LC: Sl1 wyib, yf, brp, sl1yo, brdecL, (sl1yo, brk) 5x, sl1yo, brdecR, sl1yo, brp, yb, sl1 wyib. 19 sts. Slide.

Row 13 DC: K1, sl1yo, brkyobrk, (sl1yo, brp) 6x, sl1yo, brkyobrk, sl1yo, k1. 23 sts. Turn.

Row 14 LC: Sl1 wyif, yb, brk, sl1yo, k1, (sl1yo, brp) 7x, sl1yo, k1, sl1yo, brk, yf, sl1 wyif. Slide.

Row 14 DC: Rep Row 8 DC.

Row 15 LC: Sl1 wyib, yf, (brp, sl1yo) 2x, brdecL, (sl1yo, brk) 3x, sl1yo, brdecR, (sl1yo, brp) 2x, yb, sl1 wyib. 19 sts. Slide.

Row 15 DC: K1, sl1yo, brk, sl1yo, brkyobrk, (sl1yo, brp) 4x, sl1yo, brkyobrk, sl1yo, brk, sl1yo, k1. 23 sts. Turn.

Row 16 LC: Sl1 wyif, yb, (brk, sl1yo) 2x, k1, (sl1yo, brp) 5x, sl1yo, k1, (sl1yo, brk) 2x, yf, sl1 wyif. Slide.

Row 16 DC: Rep Row 6 DC.

Row 17 LC: Sl1 wyib, yf, (brp, sl1yo) 3x, brdecL, sl1yo, brk, sl1yo, brdecR, (sl1yo, brp) 3x, yb, sl1 wyib. 19 sts. Slide.

Row 17 DC: K1, (sl1yo, brk) 2x, sl1yo, brkyobrk, (sl1yo, brp) 2x, sl1yo, brkyobrk, (sl1yo, brk) 2x, sl1yo, k1. 23 sts. Turn.

Row 18 LC: Sl1 wyif, yb, (brk, sl1yo) 3x, k1, (sl1yo, brp) 3x, sl1yo, k1, (sl1yo, brk) 3x, yf, sl1 wyif. Slide.

Row 18 DC: Rep Row 2 DC.

Row 19 LC: Sl1 wyib, yf, (brp, sl1yo) 4x, br4stdec, (sl1yo, brp) 4x, yb, sl1 wyib. 19 sts. Slide.

Row 19 DC: K1, (sl1yo, brk) 2x, sl1yo, brkyobrk, sl1yo, brdecL, sl1yo, brkyobrk, (sl1yo, brk) 2x, sl1yo, k1. 21 sts. Turn.

Row 20 LC: Sl1 wyif, yb, (brk, sl1yo) 3x, k1, sl1yo, (brk, sl1yo) 2x, k1, (sl1yo, brk) 3x, yf, sl1 wyif. Slide.

Row 20 DC: P1, (sl1yo, brp) 9x, sl1yo, p1. Turn.

Row 21 LC: Sl1 wyib, yf, (brp, sl1yo) 9x, brp, yb, sl1 wyib. Slide. Cut CC, leaving 6"/15 cm tail.

Row 21 DC: K1, (p1, brk) 9x, p1, k1. Turn.

FINISHING

With WS facing, BO in ribbing pattern using Jeny's Surprisingly Stretchy Bind Off (see Special Techniques). Sew in ends. Wet block to desired shape. (The leafy pattern may want to pull in at the sides; wet blocking will help achieve a square coaster.)

Latte Leaf Cup Cozy with Latte Leaf Coaster

DIRECTIONS: LATTE LEAF CUP COZY

With DC, CO 36 sts using Long Tail Cast On. PM, join to work in the round. Knit 1 round.

> **TIP** If you're using magic loop or 2 circular needles, put the first 21 sts on the one needle, so your leaf knitting is uninterrupted on one needle.

Setup Rnd (DC): *K1, sl1yo; rep from * to end. Drop DC at front of work without creating the final yo; it will hang between last 2 sts of rnd. All DC rnds end this way. Last st of rnd is missing its yo; it will get its yo at end of next rnd. (This is the "delayed" gratification method of handling your beginning/end of rnd as described on page 26, with colors reversed.)

> **TIP** Temporarily tie the ends of DC and LC together when beginning Rnd 1, so you don't lose the yo of the first sl1yo.

Work Latte Leaf Cup Cozy pattern from written instructions or chart. (See chart on next page.)

Rnd 1 LC: Join LC. *Sl1yo, brp; rep from * to end. To brp the last st, lift DC over left needle; this is the missing yo from previous rnd. Brp into this st and its yo. Drop DC in back of work. All LC rnds end this way. Pick up DC and begin next rnd.

Rnd 1 DC: *Brk, sl1yo; rep from * to end.

Rnd 2 LC: Rep Rnd 1 LC.

Rnd 2 DC: (Brk, sl1yo) 5x, (brp, sl1yo) 2x, *brk, sl1yo; rep from * to end.

Rnd 3 LC: (Sl1yo, brp) 5x, sl1yo, br4st inc, *sl1yo, brp; rep from * to end. 40 sts.

Rnd 3 DC: (Brk, sl1yo) 4x, brdecR, (sl1yo, p1) 2x, sl1yo, brdecL, sl1yo, *brk, sl1yo; rep from * to end. 36 sts.

Rnd 4 LC: (Sl1yo, brp) 4x, (sl1yo, brk) 3x, *sl1yo, brp; rep from * to end.

Rnd 4 DC: Rep Rnd 2 DC.

Rnd 5 LC: (Sl1yo, brp) 4x, sl1yo, brk, sl1yo, br4st inc, sl1yo, brk, *sl1yo, brp; rep from * to end. 40 sts.

Rnd 5 DC: (Brk, sl1yo) 3x, brdecR, sl1yo, brp, (sl1yo, p1) 2x, sl1yo, brp, sl1yo, brdecL, sl1yo, *brk, sl1yo; rep from * to end. 36 sts.

Rnd 6 LC: (Sl1yo, brp) 3x, (sl1yo, brk) 5x, *sl1yo, brp; rep from * to end.

Rnd 6 DC: (Brk, sl1yo) 4x, (brp, sl1yo) 4x, *brk, sl1yo; rep from * to end.

Rnd 7 LC: (Sl1yo, brp) 3x, (sl1yo, brk) 2x, sl1yo, br4st inc, (sl1yo, brk) 2x, *sl1yo, brp; rep from * to end. 40 sts.

Rnd 7 DC: (Brk, sl1yo) 2x, brdecR, (sl1yo, brp) 2x, (sl1yo, p1) 2x, (sl1yo, brp) 2x, sl1yo, brdecL, sl1yo, *brk, sl1yo; rep from * to end. 36 sts.

Rnd 8 LC: (Sl1yo, brp) 2x, (sl1yo, brk) 7x, *sl1yo, brp; rep from * to end.

Rnd 8 DC: (Brk, sl1yo) 2x, brk, (sl1yo, brp) 6x, sl1yo, *brk, sl1yo; rep from * to end.

Rnds 9 LC & DC – 10 LC & DC: Rep [Rnds 8 LC & DC] twice.

Rnd 11 LC: (Sl1yo, brp) 2x, sl1yo, brdecL, (sl1yo, brk) 3x, sl1yo, brdecR, *sl1yo, brp; rep from * to end. 32 sts.

LATTE LEAF CUP COZY CHART

KEY

(white box)	white
(box)	knit
•	purl
∩	brk
⋒	brp
‖	sl1yo
⤒	brdecR
⋀	brdecL
⋒⋒⋒	brkyobrk
⋒⋒⋒⋒	br4st inc
⋀⋀	br4stdec
✕	no stitch
(light box)	Syncopated LC
(shaded box)	Syncopated DC
(box)	Brioche Rib repeat
(box)	Setup Round
(box)	LC
(shaded box)	DC

Chart column headers (top and bottom): 24 23 22 21 20 19 18 17 16 15 14 13 12 11 10 9 8 7 6 5 4 3 2 1

Row labels (bottom to top): 1 LC, 1 DC, 2 LC, 2 DC, 3 LC, 3 DC, 4 LC, 4 DC, 5 LC, 5 DC, 6 LC, 6 DC, 7 LC, 7 DC, 8 LC, 8 DC, 9 LC, 9 DC, 10 LC, 10 DC, 11 LC, 11 DC, 12 LC, 12 DC, 13 LC, 13 DC, 14 LC, 14 DC, 15 LC, 15 DC, 16 LC, 16 DC, 17 LC, 17 DC

Rnd 11 DC: (Brk, sl1yo) 2x, brkyobrk, (sl1yo, brp) 4x, sl1yo, brkyobrk, sl1yo, *brk, sl1yo; rep from * to end. 36 sts.

Rnd 12 LC: (Sl1yo, brp) 2x, sl1yo, p1, (sl1yo, brk) 5x, sl1yo, p1, *sl1yo, brp; rep from * to end.

Rnd 12 DC: Rep Rnd 6 DC.

Rnd 13 LC: (Sl1yo, brp) 3x, sl1yo, brdecL, sl1yo, brk, sl1yo, brdecR, *sl1yo, brp; rep from * to end. 32 sts.

Rnd 13 DC: (Brk, sl1yo) 3x, brkyobrk, (sl1yo, brp) 2x, sl1yo, brkyobrk, sl1yo, *brk, sl1yo; rep from * to end. 36 sts.

Rnd 14 LC: (Sl1yo, brp) 3x, sl1yo, p1, (sl1yo, brk) 3x, sl1yo, p1, *sl1yo, brp; rep from * to end.

Rnd 14 DC: Rep Rnd 2 DC.

Rnd 15 LC: (Sl1yo, brp) 4x, sl1yo, br4stdec, *sl1yo, brp; rep from * to end. 32 sts.

Rnd 15 DC: (Brk, sl1yo) 3x, brkyobrk, sl1yo, brdecL, sl1yo, brkyobrk, sl1yo, *brk, sl1yo; rep from * to end. 34 sts.

Rnd 16 LC: Sl1yo, brp, [(sl1yo, brp) 2x, sl1yo, p1] 2x, *sl1yo, brp; rep from * to end.

Rnd 16 DC: *Brk, sl1yo; rep from * to end.

Rnd 17 LC: *Sl1yo, brp; rep from * to end. Cut CC, leaving 6"/15 cm tail.

Rnd 17 DC: *Brk, p1; rep from * to end.

With DC, knit 1 rnd.

FINISHING

BO all sts loosely knitwise using Suspended Bind Off (see Special Techniques). You're aiming for a bind off loose enough to go around your cup, but tight enough to help keep your cup from sliding through the cozy. I used a needle 2 sizes larger for the bind off. Sew in ends. Wet block to desired shape.

Latte Leaf Cup Cozy with Latte Leaf Coasters

CHAPTER 7

Putting it All Together

We've come a long way on our brioche journey, from the simplest one color brioche, on up through two color brioche, syncopation, and increases and decreases. Let's put all these new skills together and take a virtual road trip for a little coffee break at the coast!

The Oregon Coast is where I go to unwind and soak up inspiration. My best ideas often come to me during long walks on the beach. Then I settle in with yarn, needles, and a cup of coffee in front of a big picture window to bring those ideas to life.

I've been organizing an annual Crafty Moms Weekend with a group of friends at the coast for the past 20 years. We each bring our own projects to work on; mine is always knitting. You'll find me in the corner chair, watching the waves as I enjoy my favorite craft.

I'm constantly inspired by the beauty of the Oregon Coast, and I love sharing it in my knitting designs. Fill your travel mug, and come knit amazing brioche with me.

Cappuccino Cowl

The peaks on this cowl remind me of the milk foam peaks that grace the top of a cappuccino. When you flip the cowl upside down; the peaks become the sky, and the espresso turns into mountains. This cowl was inspired by the peaks of the Coast Range that lies between the Willamette River Valley and the Oregon Coast. With travel mugs in hand, we'll venture through the mountains as dappled light filters through the towering evergreen trees.

This cowl is worked in the round from the top down, from foam to espresso (sky to mountains). The peaks are created with syncopated Brioche Rib. Each round is worked twice, first with LC and then with DC.

TIP Remember to move your syncopation markers before each odd numbered round when knitting the syncopated brioche section. See instructions at top of page 88.

YARN
Worsted weight yarn in 2 contrasting colors | Shown in Malabrigo Rios (100% Superwash Wool, 210 yards/192 meters in 100 g), 1 skein each color Aguas (DC) and Cosmos (LC) | 93 yards/85 meters DC and 88 yards/81 meters LC

NEEDLES
US 6/4.0 mm 24"/60 cm circular needle, or size to attain gauge or a fabric you like

GAUGE
18 sts in 4"/10 cm in Brioche Rib worked in the round, after blocking | Gauge not critical

NOTIONS
Tapestry needle
Stitch markers (6) (4 of these should be removable locking stitch markers for marking syncopation points)

FINISHED SIZE
22"/56 cm circumference, 6"/15 cm tall

DIRECTIONS
With LC, CO 100 sts using Long Tail Cast On. PM (unique marker for BOR), join to work in the round. Knit 1 round.

Setup Rnd LC: *K1, sl1yo; rep from * to end.
Setup Rnd DC: Join DC. *Sl1yo, brp; rep from * to end.

LC BRIOCHE RIB
Rnd 1 LC: *Brk, sl1yo; rep from * to end.
Rnd 1 DC: *Sl1yo, brp; rep from * to end.

Rep [Rnds 1 LC & DC] 7 more times (8 LC and 8 DC rnds total), ending with Rnd 1 DC.

CAPPUCCINO COWL SYNCOPATED BRIOCHE
Before beginning the written or charted instructions, place markers for Cappuccino Syncopated Brioche Chart as follows: Place a Repeat Marker between 50th and 51st st of rnd; 50 st pattern is worked twice over 100 sts. Place Peak1 Markers before and after 16th st in each 50 st section. I like to use a green marker where the mountain peak starts, and a red marker where it ends, to differentiate the two. Mountain peaks grow 4 sts wider on each odd numbered round, 2 sts on each side of the peak's central stitch.

CAPPUCCINO COWL SYNCOPATED BRIOCHE CHART

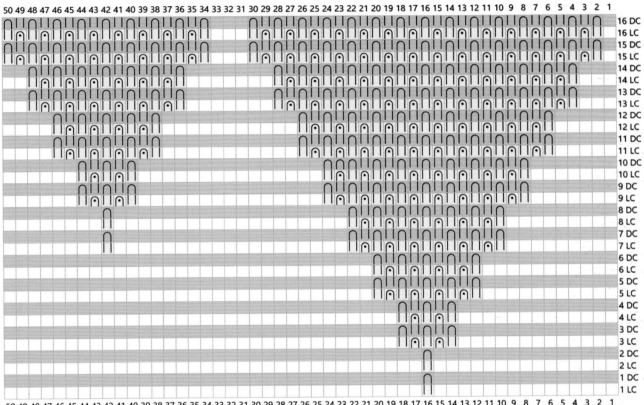

KEY

⌂ brk   ⌂ brp   ‖ sl1yo

☐ LC rnd   ▨ DC rnd   ☐ Syncopated LC

▨ Syncopated DC

Work Cappuccino Syncopated Brioche from written instructions or chart. **For all knitters:** Make sure you have placed your markers carefully before beginning this section. **After Rnd 1, remember to move Peak Markers before each odd numbered rnd**, to prepare for next syncopation shift. You'll move them 2 sts to the left and right of each mountain peak. Markers for Peak2 are added before beginning Rnd 7, before and after 42nd st.

The chart begins on a background of LC Brioche Rib as established; only the syncopated green shaded sections show the brioche stitches. Continue LC Brioche Rib outside of the syncopated mountains.

CAPPUCCINO COWL SYNCOPATED BRIOCHE

Rnd 1 LC: *(Brk, sl1yo) 7x, brk, sm, sl1yo, sm, (brk, sl1yo) 17x to Repeat Marker; rep from * once more to end of rnd.

Rnd 1 DC: *(Sl1yo, brp) 7x, sl1yo, sm, brk, sm, (sl1yo, brp) 17x to Repeat Marker; rep from * once more to end of rnd.

Rnds 2 LC & DC, and all even rnds through 16 LC & DC: Rep immediately previous Rnds LC & DC. Example: for Rnds 2 LC & DC, rep Rnds 1 LC & DC.

Rnd 3 LC: *(Brk, sl1yo) 6x, brk, sm, (sl1yo, brp) 2x, sl1yo, sm, (brk, sl1yo) 16x to Repeat Marker; rep from * once more to end of rnd.

Rnd 3 DC: *(Sl1yo, brp) 6x, sl1yo, sm, (brk, sl1yo) 2x, brk, sm, (sl1yo, brp) 16x to Repeat Marker; rep from * once more to end of rnd.

Rnd 5 LC: *(Brk, sl1yo) 5x, brk, sm, (sl1yo, brp) 4x, sl1yo, sm, (brk, sl1yo) 15x to Repeat Marker; rep from * once more to end of rnd.

Rnd 5 DC: *(Sl1yo, brp) 5x, sl1yo, sm, (brk, sl1yo) 4x, brk, sm, (sl1yo, brp) 15x to Repeat Marker; rep from * once more to end of rnd.

Rnd 7 LC: *(Brk, sl1yo) 4x, brk, sm, (sl1yo, brp) 6x, sl1yo, sm, brk, (sl1yo, brk) 9x, place first Peak2 Marker, sl1yo, place second Peak2 Marker, (brk, sl1yo) 4x to Repeat Marker; rep from * once more to end of rnd.

Rnd 7 DC: *(Sl1yo, brp) 4x, sl1yo, sm, (brk, sl1yo) 6x, brk, sm, sl1yo, (brp, s1yo) 9x, sm, brk, sm, (sl1yo, brp) 4x to Repeat Marker; rep from * once more to end of rnd.

Rnd 9 LC: *(Brk, sl1yo) 3x, brk, sm, (sl1yo, brp) 8x, sl1yo, sm, (brk, sl1yo) 7x, brk, sm, (sl1yo, brp) 2x, sl1yo, sm, (brk, sl1yo) 3x to Repeat Marker; rep from * once more to end of rnd.

Rnd 9 DC: *(Sl1yo, brp) 3x, sl1yo, sm, (brk, sl1yo) 8x, brk, sm, (sl1yo, brp) 7x, s1yo, sm, (brk, sl1yo) 2x, brk, sm, (sl1yo, brp) 3x to Repeat Marker; rep from * once more to end of rnd.

Rnd 11 LC: *(Brk, sl1yo) 2x, brk, sm, (sl1yo, brp) 10x, sl1yo, sm, (brk, sl1yo) 5x, brk, sm, (sl1yo, brp) 4x, sl1yo, sm, (brk, sl1yo) 2x to Repeat Marker; rep from * once more to end of rnd.

Rnd 11 DC: *(Sl1yo, brp) 2x, sl1yo, sm, (brk, sl1yo) 10x, brk, sm, (sl1yo, brp) 5x, sl1yo, sm, (brk, sl1yo) 4x, brk, sm, (sl1yo, brp) 2x to Repeat Marker; rep from * once more to end of rnd.

Rnd 13 LC: *Brk, sl1yo, brk, sm, (sl1yo, brp) 12x, sl1yo, sm, (brk, sl1yo) 3x, brk, sm, (sl1yo, brp) 6x, sl1yo, sm, brk, sl1yo to Repeat Marker; rep from * once more to end of rnd.

Rnd 13 DC: *Sl1yo, brp, sl1yo, sm, (brk, sl1yo) 12x, brk, sm, (sl1yo, brp) 3x, s1yo, sm, (brk, sl1yo) 6x, brk, sm, sl1yo, brp to Repeat Marker; rep from * once more to end of rnd.

NOTE: Second Peak2 Marker will overlap with end of repeat/round marker on Rnds 15 and 16; keep them to remind you where you are.

Rnd 15 LC: *Brk, sm, (sl1yo, brp) 14x, sl1yo, sm, brk, sl1yo, brk, sm, (sl1yo, brp) 8x, sl1yo to Repeat Marker; rep from * once more to end of rnd.

Rnd 15 DC: *Sl1yo, sm, (brk, sl1yo) 14x, brk, sm, sl1yo, brp, sl1yo, sm, (brk, sl1yo) 8x, brk to Repeat Marker; rep from * once more to end of rnd.

Rnds 16 LC & DC: Rep Rnds 15 LC & DC.

Mountains are complete after Rnds 16 LC & DC. Remove Peak Markers and Repeat Marker; BOR marker remains. Continue in DC Brioche Rib.

DC BRIOCHE RIB
Rnd 1 LC: *Brp, sl1yo; rep from *to end.

Rnd 1 DC: *Sl1yo, brk; rep from * to end. (Leave DC in back of work at end of rnd.)

Rep [Rnds 1 LC & DC] 7 more times (8 LC and 8 DC rnds total), ending with Rnd 1 DC.

Cut LC, leaving 6"/15 cm tail.

Closing Rnd DC: *Brk, k1; rep from * to end.

FINISHING
Knit one more round. BO all sts knitwise using Suspended Bind Off (see Special Techniques). Sew in ends. Steam or wet block.

Cappuccino Cowl

Seafoam Latte Scarf

There's nothing better than a walk on the beach. The ever-changing blues and greens of the water and the rolling whitecapped waves are an instant mood-lifter. The gentle froth at the very edge of the waves on the beach is as delicate as latte foam. Finding shells or sand dollars along the way are a bonus!

Brioche increases and decreases create Seafoam Latte's rhythmic waves. Syncopating the third wave makes the breaking crest of the wave. This project uses all your new brioche skills: two-color flat brioche with increases, decreases, and syncopation. MC is the color of the water, and CC is the color of the breaking wave.

YARN

Worsted weight yarn in 2 contrasting colors | Shown in Knit Picks Chroma Worsted (70% Superwash Wool, 30% Nylon; 198 yards/181 meters in 100 g) 1 ball each color Surf's Up (MC) and Bare (CC) | 190 yards/174 meters of each color

NEEDLES

US 6/4.0 mm 24"/60 cm circular needle, or size to attain gauge or a fabric you like

GAUGE

18.5 sts in 4"/10 cm in Brioche Rib worked flat, before blocking | Gauge not critical

NOTIONS

Tapestry needle
2 stitch markers (2 different colors)

FINISHED SIZE

6"/15 cm wide x 59"/150 cm long after blocking. (I laid it out wet to 7"/18 cm x 64"/162.5 cm and it dried to finished measurement.)

DIRECTIONS

With CC, CO 33 sts using Long Tail Cast On. Work Seafoam Latte pattern from written instructions or chart. (See chart on next page.)

Setup Row 1 CC (WS): (P1, sl1yo) 6x, pm to note syncopation point, (k1, sl1yo) 5x, pm to note repeat, (k1, sl1yo) 5x, k1. Slide work back to beginning of row. Slip repeat marker as you come to it; I'm only going to refer to the syncopation point marker from here on.

Setup Row 2 MC (WS): Sl1 wyif, yb, brk, (sl1yo, brk) 5x, sm, (sl1yo, brp) 10x, yb, sl1 wyib. Turn work.

Row 1 CC (RS): P1, (sl1yo, brp) 10x, sm, sl1yo, brkyobrk, sl1yo, brdecL, (sl1yo, brk) 2x, sl1yo, k1. Slide.

Row 1 MC (RS): Sl1 wyif, yb, *brkyobrk, sl1yo, brdecL, (sl1yo, brk) 2x, sl1yo; rep from *once, sm, brp, sl1yo, p1, (sl1yo, brp) 4x, yb, sl1 wyib. Turn.

Row 2 CC (WS): P1, (sl1yo, brp) 5x, sl1yo, sm, *(brk, sl1yo) 4x, k1, sl1yo; rep from * to last st, k1. Slide.

Row 2 MC (WS): Sl1 wyif, yb, brk, (sl1yo, brk) 5x, sm, (sl1yo, brp) 10x, yb, sl1 wyib. Turn.

SEAFOAM LATTE SCARF CHART

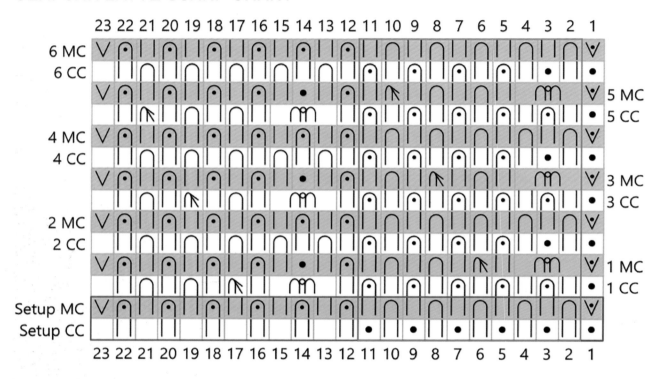

KEY

☐ RS: knit WS: purl	• RS: purl WS: knit	ⱽ RS: sl1 wyib WS: sl1 wyif
ⱽ̇ RS: sl1 wyif WS: sl1 wyib	∩ RS: brk WS: brp	⌐•⌐ RS: brp WS: brk
‖ sl1yo	⋔ brkyobrk	⋀ RS: brdecL

☐ MC feature, work 2x

☐ Setup rows

☐ CC Row

▨ MC row

Row 3 CC: P1, (sl1yo, brp) 10x, sm, sl1yo, brkyobrk, sl1yo, brk, sl1yo, brdecL, sl1yo, brk, sl1yo, k1. Slide.

Row 3 MC: Sl1 wyif, yb, *brkyobrk, sl1yo, brk, sl1yo, brdecL, sl1yo, brk, sl1yo; rep from * once, sm, brp, sl1yo, p1, (sl1yo, brp) 4x, yb, sl1 wyib. Turn.

Rows 4 CC & MC: Rep Rows 2 CC & MC.

Row 5 CC: P1, (sl1yo, brp) 10x, sm, sl1yo, brkyobrk, (sl1yo, brk) 2x, sl1yo, brdecL, sl1yo, k1. Slide.

Row 5 MC: Sl1 wyif, yb, *brkyobrk, (sl1yo, brk) 2x, sl1yo, brdecL, sl1yo; rep from * once, sm, brp, sl1yo, p1, (sl1yo, brp) 4x, yb sl1 wyib. Turn.

Rows 6 CC & MC: Rep Rows 2 CC & MC.

Rep [Rows 1 CC & MC – 6 CC & MC] 37 more times or to desired length, ending with Row 6 MC. Cut MC, leaving 6"/15 cm tail.

FINISHING
Using CC, BO in ribbing pattern, working brk into the sl1yos and p the single purl stitches. Sew in ends. Steam or wet block.

Seafoam Latte Scarf

Seagull Flight Shawl

A flight can be many things: a flight of fancy, a flight of coffee drinks, birds in flight. As we walk along the water's edge, hands wrapped around a warm cup, the gathered seagulls take wing. The Pacific Ocean and startling blue sky are the perfect backdrop. But skies and oceans don't have to be blue. What color will yours be?

Seagull Flight is a half pi shawl that features syncopated Brioche Rib and brioche increases and decreases. The seagulls are created by adding simple increases and decreases to the Brioche Rib pattern every four rows. The shawl is shaped by increasing at pre-planned intervals rather than on every row, making it a relaxing, easy to follow knit.

TIPS Gauge is not critical in this piece, but it will affect how much yarn you use.

I've included notes on how to maximize your yarn usage when you're nearing the end of the shawl.

YARN
Fingering weight yarn in 2 contrasting colors | Shown in Huckleberry Knits Gradient (75% Superwash Merino, 25% nylon, 463 yards/423 meters in 100 g) in Echo (DC) and MadelineTosh Twist Light (75% Superwash Merino, 25% nylon, 420 yards/384 meters in 100g) in Sky Wash (LC) 420 yards/384 meters DC and 375 yards/343 meters CC For a larger shawl, use 2 skeins LC and 2 skeins DC; see instructions in Seagull Flight section

NEEDLES
US 4/3.5 mm 24 or 32"/ 60 or 80 cm circular needle, or size to attain gauge or a fabric you like

GAUGE
15 sts in 4 in/10 cm in Brioche Rib worked flat, before blocking | Gauge not critical

NOTIONS
Tapestry needle
Stitch markers (30)

FINISHED SIZE
28"/71 cm back depth, 56"/142 wide across the top, blocked. For comparison purposes, 21"/53.5 cm back depth, 42"/107 cm wide across the top, unblocked.

Seagull Flight Shawl with flight of coffee

DIRECTIONS

GARTER TAB CENTER

With DC, CO 3 sts using Long Tail Cast On. Knit 6 rows.

Row 1 (RS): K3, rotate work 90 degrees, pick up and knit 3 sts along side edge (1 st in each garter bump), rotate work 90 degrees, pick up and knit 3 sts along CO edge. 9 sts.

Row 2 (WS): K3, pm, p3, pm, k3.

This 9 st "garter tab" is the foundation of the shawl. The first and last 3 sts of each row form the garter st edges; they will always be K sts. The body of the shawl grows from the 3 center sts. St counts do not include the garter st edges.

Row 3: K3, sm, yo, kfb, yo, k1, yo, kfb, yo, sm, k3. 9 sts in body.

Rows 4, 6 and 8: Knit across.

Row 5: Knit across.

Row 7: K3, sm, *k1, yo; rep from * to m, sm, k3. 18 sts in body.

Rows 9 – 14: Knit across.

Row 15: K3, sm, *k1, yo; rep from * to m, sm, k3. 36 sts in body.

Row 16: K3, sm, purl across to m, sm, k3.

LC BRIOCHE RIB

Section begins with 36 sts in body of shawl.

Setup Row 1 LC (RS): Sl3 purlwise, sm, join LC, *k1, sl1yo; rep from * to m, sm, sl3 wyif. (The final sl1yo gets its yo, and then the yarn is dropped in front so you can sl3 wyif.) Do not turn. Slide work back to beginning of row. Skip to Row 1 DC. On subsequent repeats, use Row 1 LC instead of this setup row.

Row 1 LC (RS): Sl3 wyib, sm, *brk, sl1yo; rep from * to m, sm, sl3 wyif. Slide.

Row 1 DC (RS): K3, sm, *sl1yo, brp; rep from * to m, sm, k3. Turn.

Row 2 LC (WS): Sl3 wyib, yf, sm, sl1yo, brp; rep from * to m, sl3 wyif. Slide.

Row 2 DC (WS): K3, sm, *brk, sl1yo; rep from * to m, sm, k3. Turn.

Rows 3 LC & DC – 10 LC & DC: Rep [Rows 1 LC & DC – 2 LC & DC] 4 more times.

Rows 11 LC & DC: Rep [Rows 1 LC & DC] once more.

Row 12 LC (WS): Rep Row 2 LC. Slide.

Closing Row DC (WS): K3, sm, *brk, p1; rep from * to m, sm, k3. Turn. (Twist LC and DC around each other at beginning of next row to carry LC up for next use.)

Inc Row DC (RS): K3, sm, *yo, k1; rep from * to m, sm, k3. 72 sts in body. Turn.

Return Row DC (WS): K3, sm, purl across to m, sm, k3. Turn.

DC BRIOCHE RIB

Section begins with 72 sts in body of shawl.

Setup Row 1 LC (RS): Sl3 wyib, yf, sm, *sl1yo, p1; rep from * to m, sm, sl3 wyif. Do not turn. Slide work back to beginning of row. Skip to Row 1 DC. On subsequent repeats, use Row 1 LC instead of this setup row.

Row 1 LC (RS): Sl3 wyib, yf, sm, *sl1yo, brp; rep from * to m, sm, sl3 wyif. Slide.

Row 1 DC (RS): K3, sm, *brk, sl1yo; rep from * to m, sm, k3. Turn.

Row 2 LC (WS): Sl3 wyib, sm, *brk, sl1yo; rep from * to m, sm, sl3 wyif. Slide.

Row 2 DC (WS): K3, sm, *sl1yo, brp; rep from * to m, sm, k3. Turn.

Rows 3 LC & DC – 22 LC & DC: Rep [Rows 1 LC & DC – 2 LC & DC] 10 more times.

Rows 23 LC & DC: Rep [Rows 1 LC & DC] once more.

Row 24 LC (WS): Rep Row 2 LC. Do not turn. Slide.

Closing Row DC (WS): K3, sm, *k1, brp; rep from * to m, sm, k3. Turn. (Twist LC and DC around each other at beginning of next row to carry LC up for next use.)

Inc Row DC (RS): K3, sm, k1, *yo, k1; rep from * to m, sm, k3. 143 sts in body. Turn.

Return Row DC (WS): K3, sm, purl across to m, sm, k3. Turn.

FIRST LC SEAGULL FLIGHT

Section begins with 143 sts in body of shawl. On rows where not specifically noted, sm as encountered. Work Seagull Flight pattern from written instructions or chart. (See chart on next page.) **For chart knitters:** The first time Row 1 LC (RS) of the 4-row Seagull Flight Pattern is worked, markers should be placed before the first 10 st repeat, and after each subsequent 10 st repeat.

Setup Row 1 LC (RS): Sl3 wyib, sm, k1, *sl1yo, k1; rep from * to m, sm, sl3 wyib. Do not turn. Slide work back to beginning of row.

Setup Row 1 DC (RS): K3, sm, sl1yo, *brp, sl1yo; rep from * to m, sm, k3. Turn.

Setup Row 2 LC (WS): Sl3 wyif, sm, brp, *sl1yo, brp; rep from * to m, sm, sl3 wyif. Slide.

Setup Row 2 DC (WS): K3, sm, sl1yo, *brk, sl1yo; rep from * to m, sm, k3. Turn.

Row 1 LC (RS): Sl3 wyib, sm, brk, sl1yo, pm, *brdecR, sl1yo, br4st inc, sl1yo, brdecL, sl1yo, pm; rep from * to last st before final m, brk, sm, sl3 wyib. Do not turn. Slide work back to beginning of row.

Row 1 DC (RS): K3, sm, sl1yo, brp, sm, *sl1yo, brp, (sl1yo, p1) 2x, (sl1yo, brp) 2x, sm; rep from * to last st before final m, sl1yo, sm, k3. Turn.

Row 2 LC (WS): Sl3 wyif, sm, brp, *sl1yo, brp; rep from * to final m, sm, sl3 wyif. Slide.

Row 2 DC (WS): K3, sm, sl1yo, *brk, sl1yo; rep from * to final m, sm, k3. Turn.

Row 3 LC (RS): Sl3 wyib, sm, brk, *sl1yo, brk; rep from * to final m, sm, sl3 wyib. Slide.

SEAGULL FLIGHT PATTERN CHART

KEY

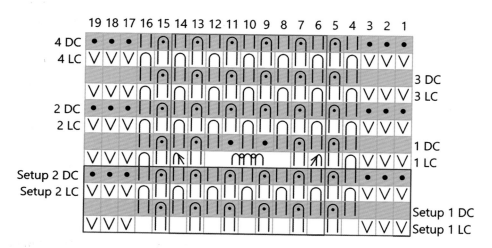

	RS: knit WS: purl
•	RS: purl WS: knit
V	RS: sl1 wyib WS: sl1 wyif
∩	RS: brk WS: brp
⋒	RS: brp WS: brk
‖	sl1yo
⟰	RS: brdecR
⋔	RS: brdecL
⋒⋒⋒	br4st inc
	Pattern repeat
	Setup Rows
	LC
(shaded)	DC

Seagull Flight Shawl back view

Row 3 DC (RS): K3, sm, sl1yo, *brp, sl1yo; rep from * to final m, sm, k3. Turn.

Rows 4 LC & DC: Rep Rows 2 LC & DC.

TIP The markers placed on Row 1 help you establish your Seagull Flight stitch pattern. If you can read your knitting, you don't need to keep these markers after a few completed 4 row repeats.

Rows 5 LC & DC – 36 LC & DC: Rep [Rows 1 LC & DC – 4 LC & DC of Seagull Flight Pattern] 8 more times.

Rows 37 LC & DC: Rep [Rows 1 LC & DC] once more.

Row 38 LC (WS): Rep Row 2 LC. Slide. Remove Seagull Flight markers on next row.

NOTE Looking to maximize your yarn usage? Weigh your yarns here, and after the 2 setup and 17 rows of the Second Seagull Flight section. Divide the resulting difference in weight by 19 to see how many grams you've used per row. The rest of the pattern as written has 12 LC rows and 17 DC rows. Do you have enough yarn? If you're running short, you can shorten your DC Brioche Rib section at the end. If you're running really short, you can end with the Seagulls Closing Row, and bind off without a DC Brioche section. If you have a lot left over, check to see if you can add an extra 4 row repeat of seagulls to the Second Seagull Flight. I had plenty of yarn, so I worked an extra 4 row Seagull Flight repeat to my Second Seagull Flight. If you're using 2 skeins of each color, work the Second Seagull Flight to be as long as the first, or longer. You can work up to 60 rows (plus closing) of the Second Seagull Flight pattern, and the DC Brioche Rib, without needing another increase row.

Closing Row DC (WS): K3, sm, brk2tog (work the p st and the following brk st all together), *p1, brk; rep from * to last st before final marker, p1, sm, k3. 1 st dec; 142 sts in body. Turn. (Twist LC and DC around each other at beginning of next row to carry LC up for next use.)

Inc Row DC (RS): K3, sm, k1, *yo, k1; rep from * to m, sm, k3. 283 sts in body. Turn.

Return Row DC (WS): K3, sm, purl across to m, sm, k3. Turn.

SECOND LC SEAGULL FLIGHT

Section begins with 283 sts in body of shawl.

Work Seagull Flight Setup Rows once.

Work 4-row Seagull Flight Pattern four times. Work Rows 1 LC & DC once.

Work Row 2 LC once. Slide. Remove Seagull Flight markers on next row.

Closing Row DC (WS): K3, sm, brk2tog (work the p st and the following brk st all together), *p1, brk; rep from * to m, sm, k3. 1 st dec; 282 sts in body. Turn. (Twist LC and DC around each other at beginning of next row to carry LC up for next use.)

Eyelet Row DC (RS): K3, sm, *k2tog, yo; rep from * to m, sm, k3. 282 sts in body. Turn.

Return Row DC (WS): K3, sm, purl across to m, sm, k3. Turn.

DC BRIOCHE RIB

Work DC Brioche Rib as before, working Setup Row 1 LC, Row 1 DC, and Rows 2 LC & DC once.

Rep Rows [1 LC & DC – 2 LC & DC] 4 more times or to desired length, ending with a WS DC row.

Work Row 1 LC once more. Cut LC, leaving 6"/15 cm tail. Do not turn. Slide.

Closing Row DC (RS): K3, sm, *brk, p1; rep from * to m, sm, K3.

FINISHING

Jeny's Surprisingly Stretchy Bind Off ensures that the Brioche Rib edging can be blocked out to its full potential. Use this between the garter st edges. To begin, with WS facing, BO 1 st conventionally. Then work Jeny's Surprisingly Stretchy Bind Off (see Special Techniques) to last 2 sts. Use conventional BO for last 2 stitches. Cut yarn leaving 6"/15 cm tail. Weave in ends, wash and block to desired dimensions.

Seagull Flight Shawl front view

Coffee Bean Trivia Cowl

It sounds like a board game, but a coffee bean trivia is a small spotted shell that is shaped like a coffee bean. You won't find them on Oregon beaches, though; they're common in the Caribbean. I found mine in the British Virgin Islands, and crocheted it into a bracelet using my Victoriana pattern, which you can find free at PDXKnitterati.com

Coffee Bean Trivia is a bandana-style cowl. It begins at the bottom point and is worked flat until it's wide enough to join to work in the round for the cowl neck. You'll work a little more trivia at the neckline, and then it's time to bind off. You can easily adjust the width of the neckline, but this will also affect the length of the bandana triangle. If you like, you can also adjust the height of the circular cowl neckline. Knitter's choice!

YARN

Fingering weight yarn in 2 contrasting colors | Shown in Hazel Knits Entice (70% Superwash Merino, 20% cashmere, 10% nylon; 400 yards/366 meters in 113 g), 1 skein each color Sapphire (DC) and Jellyfish (LC) | 180 yards/165 meters DC and 190 yards/174 meters LC

NEEDLES

US 4/3.5 mm 24"/60 cm circular needle, or size to attain gauge or a fabric you like (you can move to a 16"/40 cm circular when knitting in the round, but I like the 24"/60 cm needle for knitting flat, for ease of measuring width of triangle)

GAUGE

23 sts and 30 rows in 4"/10 cm in Coffee Bean Trivia stitch pattern worked flat, after blocking | Gauge not critical

NOTIONS

Tapestry needle
Stitch markers

FINISHED SIZE

18.5"/47 cm long, 21"/53 cm wide at neckline edge, steam blocked. Cowl neck circumference is 21"/53 cm and 4.5"/11.5 cm tall.

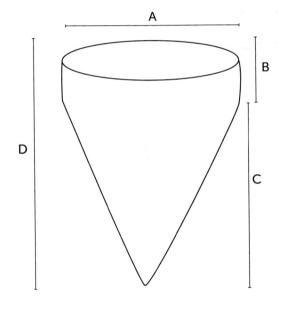

A. 21"/53 cm
C. 14"/36 cm
B. 4.5"/11.5 cm
D. 18.5"/47 cm

COFFEE BEAN TRIVIA BEGINNING TRIANGLE CHART

KEY

	RS: knit / WS: purl
	RS: purl / WS: knit
	sl1yo
	RS: brp / WS: brk
	RS: brk / WS: brp
	RS: sl1 wyib / WS: sl1 wyif
	RS: brdecL
mmm	br4st inc
mm	brkyobrk
	Setup rows
	Center Trivia motif
	LC
	DC

DIRECTIONS

With LC, CO 9 sts using Long Tail Cast On. Work Coffee Bean Trivia Beginning Triangle pattern from written instructions or chart.

Setup Row LC (WS): P1, *sl1yo, p1; rep from * to end. 9 sts. Slide work back to beginning of row.

Setup Row DC (WS): Sl1 wyif, yb, (brk, sl1yo) 3x, brk, yf, sl1 wyif. Turn work.

Row 1 LC (RS): K1, sl1yo, brk, sl1yo, br4st inc, sl1yo, brk, sl1yo, k1. 13 sts. Slide.

Row 1 DC (RS): Sl1 wyib, yf, (brp, sl1yo) 2x, (p1, sl1yo) 2x, brp, sl1yo, brp, yb, sl1 wyib. Turn.

Row 2 LC and all even LC Rows (WS): P1, *sl1yo, brp; rep from * to last 2 sts, sl1yo, p1. Slide.

Row 2 DC and all even DC Rows (WS): Sl1 wyif, yb, *brk, sl1yo; rep from * to last 2 sts, brk, yf, sl1 wyif. Turn.

Row 3 LC: K1, sl1yo, brkyobrk, (sl1yo, brk) 3x, sl1yo, brkyobrk, sl1yo, k1. 17 sts. Slide.

Row 3 DC: Sl1 wyib, yf, brp, sl1yo, p1, (sl1yo, brp) 4x, sl1yo, p1, sl1yo, brp, yb, sl1 wyib. Turn.

Row 5 LC: K1, sl1yo, brkyobrk, sl1yo, brk, sl1yo, brkyobrk, sl1yo, brdecL, sl1yo, brk, sl1yo, brkyobrk, sl1yo, k1. 21 sts. Slide.

Row 5 DC: Sl1 wyib, yf, brp, sl1yo, p1, (sl1yo, brp) 2x, sl1yo, p1, (sl1yo, brp) 3x, sl1yo, p1, sl1yo, brp, yb, sl1 wyib. Turn.

Row 7 LC: K1, sl1yo, brkyobrk, (sl1yo, brk) 2x, sl1yo, brkyobrk, sl1yo, brdecL, (sl1yo, brk) x 2, sl1yo, brkyobrk, sl1yo, k1. 25 sts. Slide.

Row 7 DC: Sl1 wyib, yf, brp, sl1yo, p1, (sl1yo, brp) 3x, sl1yo, p1, (sl1yo, brp) 4x, sl1yo, p1, sl1yo, brp, yb, sl1 wyib. Turn.

Row 9 LC: K1, *sl1yo, brk; rep from * to last 2 sts, sl1yo, k1. Slide.

Row 9 DC: Sl1 wyib, yf, *brp, sl1yo; rep from * to last 2 sts, brp, yb, sl1 wyib. Turn.

Rows 10 LC & DC: Rep Rows 2 LC & DC.

COFFEE BEAN TRIVIA BODY

Body begins with 25 sts from Coffee Bean Trivia Beginning Triangle. Each 12-row repeat of the Coffee Bean Trivia Body pattern adds 12 sts to body, 6 sts on each side of center motif. At the beginning of each repeat, add markers and incorporate both sets of new sts into another 6-st repeat on each side. (Chart knitters: Place first markers on each side of 6-stitch center Trivia motif.)

Work Coffee Bean Trivia Body pattern from written instructions or chart. (See chart on next page.)

Row 1 LC (RS): K1, sl1yo, brkyobrk, sl1yo, pm, *brdecR, sl1yo, brkyobrk, sl1yo, pm (sm on subsequent rows); rep from * to last 3 sts, brkyobrk, sl1yo, k1. 4 st inc. Slide.

Row 1 DC (RS): Sl1 wyib, yf, brp, sl1yo, p1, sl1yo, brp, sm, *sl1yo, brp, sl1yo, p1, sl1yo, brp, sm; rep from * to last 5 sts, sl1yo, p1, sl1yo, brp, yb, sl1 wyib. Turn.

Row 2 LC and all even LC Rows (WS): P1, *sl1yo, brp; rep from * to last 2 sts, sl1yo, p1. Slide.

Row 2 DC and all even DC Rows (WS): Sl1 wyif, yb, *brk, sl1yo; rep from * to last 2 sts, brk, yf, sl1 wyif. Turn.

Row 3 LC: K1, (sl1yo, brk) 2x, sl1yo, sm, *brdecR, sl1yo, brkyobrk, sl1yo, sm; rep from * to last 5 sts, (brk, sl1yo) 2x, k1. Slide.

Row 3 DC: Sl1 wyib, yf, (brp, sl1yo) 2x, brp, sm, *sl1yo, brp, sl1yo, p1, sl1yo, brp, sm; rep from * to last 5 sts, (sl1yo, brp) 2x, yb, sl1 wyib. Turn.

Row 5 LC: K1, sl1yo, brkyobrk, sl1yo, brk, sl1yo, sm, *(brk, sl1yo) 3x, sm; rep from * to last 5 sts, brk, sl1yo, brkyobrk, sl1yo, k1. 4 sts inc. Slide.

Row 5 DC: Sl1 wyib, yf, brp, sl1yo, p1, (sl1yo, brp) 2x, sm, *(sl1yo, brp) 3x, sm; rep from * to last 7 sts, sl1yo, brp, sl1yo, p1, sl1yo, brp, yb, sl1 wyib. Turn.

Row 7 LC: K1, (sl1yo, brk) 3x, sl1yo, sm, *brkyobrk, sl1yo, brdecL, sl1yo, sm; rep from * to last 7 sts, (brk, sl1yo) 3x, k1. Slide.

Row 7 DC: Sl1 wyib, yf, (brp, sl1yo) 3x, brp, sm, *sl1yo, p1, (sl1yo, brp) 2x, sm; rep from * to last 7 sts, (sl1yo, brp) 3x, yb, sl1 wyib. Turn.

COFFEE BEAN TRIVIA BODY CHART

KEY

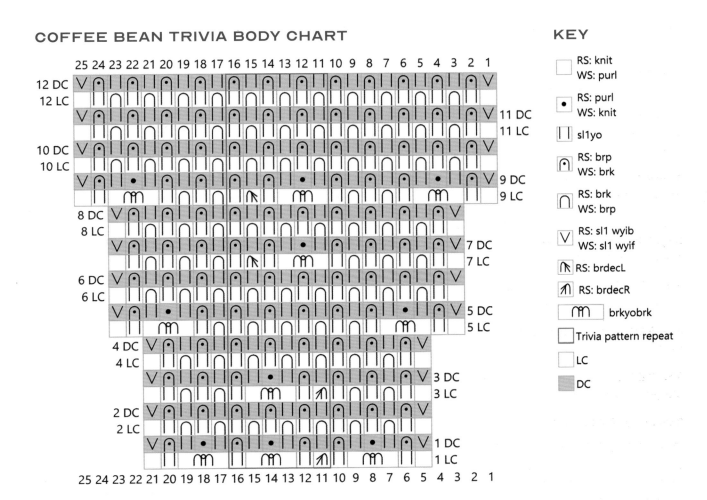

	KEY
☐	RS: knit / WS: purl
•	RS: purl / WS: knit
‖	sl1yo
⋒	RS: brp / WS: brk
⋃	RS: brk / WS: brp
V	RS: sl1 wyib / WS: sl1 wyif
⋀	RS: brdecL
⋀	RS: brdecR
⋔⋔	brkyobrk
☐	Trivia pattern repeat
☐	LC
▨	DC

Row 9 LC: K1, sl1yo, brkyobrk, (sl1yo, brk) 2x, sl1yo, sm, *brkyobrk, sl1yo, brdecL, sl1yo, sm; rep from * to last 7 sts, (brk, sl1yo) 2x, brkyobrk, sl1yo, k1. 4 sts inc. Slide.

Row 9 DC: Sl1 wyib, yf, brp, sl1yo, p1, (sl1yo, brp) 3x, sm, *sl1yo, p1, (sl1yo, brp) 2x, sm; rep from * to last 9 sts, (sl1yo, brp) 2x, sl1yo, p1, sl1yo, brp, yb, sl1 wyib. Turn.

Row 11 LC: K1, *sl1yo, brk; rep from * to last 2 sts, sl1yo, k1. Slide.

Row 11 DC: Sl1 wyib, yf, *brp, sl1yo; rep from * to last 2 sts, brp, yb, sl1 wyib. Turn.

Rows 12 LC & DC: Rep Rows 2 LC & DC.

Rep [Rows 1 LC & DC – 12 LC & DC] 6 more times, then work [Rows 1 LC & DC – 10 LC & DC] once more. 121 sts. Piece should measure about 21″/53 cm wide at the top edge and 14″/35.5 cm long. If the top edge isn't wide enough, work an additional rep of [Rows 1 LC – 12 DC] before working final 10 rows; at the project gauge, this additional repeat would allow the piece to measure 23″/66 cm wide and 16″/41 cm long. The width will be the circumference of the cowl's neckline.

JOINING TO WORK IN THE ROUND

Joining Rnd 1 LC (RS): K1, sl1yo, brk, sl1yo, pm, *brk, sl1yo; rep from * to last 3 sts, pm (this will be BOR), brk, sl1yo, k2tog (first and last st) to join in the rnd. 120 sts. Slip last 3 sts from RH needle back to LH needle purlwise.

Joining Rnd 1 DC: *Sl1yo, brp; rep from * to end.

Transition Rnd 2 LC: *Brk, sl1yo; rep from * to end.

Transition Rnd 2 DC: *Sl1yo, brp; rep from * to end.

Beginning with Row 1 LC of the Coffee Bean Trivia Body chart, work *only* the 6-st repeat portion of the Coffee Bean Trivia pattern from chart or written instructions below. The 6-st repeat is worked 20 times over the 120 sts of the cowl neck. Remember that you are now working in the round, so RS is always facing you. For chart knitters: read all rows from right to left.

Rnd 1 LC: *BrdecR, sl1yo, brkyobrk, sl1yo; rep from * to end.

Rnd 1 DC: *Sl1yo, brp, sl1yo, p1, sl1yo, brp; rep from * to end.

Rnd 2 LC & all even LC Rnds: *Brk, sl1yo; rep from * to end.

Rnd 2 DC & all even DC Rnds: *Sl1yo, brp; rep from * to end.

Rnds 3 LC & DC: Rep Rnds 1 LC & DC.

Rnds 5 LC & DC: Rep Rnds 2 LC & DC

Rnd 7 LC: *Brkyobrk, sl1yo, brdecL, sl1yo; rep from * to end.

Rnd 7 DC: *Sl1yo, p1, (sl1yo, brp) 2x; rep from * to end.

Rnds 9 LC & DC: Rep Rnds 7 LC & DC.

Rnds 11 LC & DC – 12 LC & DC: Rep [Rnds 2 LC & DC] twice.

Rep [Rnds 1 LC & DC – 12 LC & DC] to desired height for cowl neck, ending with Rnd 1 DC or 7 DC. Cowl shown has [Rnds 1 LC & DC – 12 LC & DC] worked twice, then Rnds [1 LC & DC] once more. Cut DC, leaving 6″/15 cm tail.

FINISHING

Closing Rnd LC: *Brk, p1; rep from * to end.

BO loosely in rib pattern using Jeny's Surprisingly Stretchy Bind Off. Sew in ends. Steam or wet block to desired measurements.

TIP A stretchy bind off is important here; you want to be able to get this over your head!

Coffee Breakers Cowl/Shawl

Is it a cowl? Is it a shawl? It's knitter's choice! Coffee Breakers can be knit as a small or large cowl, or a shawl. The big rolling wave on the edge of this piece invites us to continue our walk along the shore. Come take a break by the breakers!

Coffee Breakers features a syncopated brioche wave edging, and a contrasting Brioche Rib body with regular increases to create an asymmetric triangle. The repeating dark Brioche Rib in the body ends at the syncopation point, when the light color wave gets its chance to shine. Knitting begins at the narrow end for all versions.

This cowl is a flattering, easy to wear shape that stays on as you move through your day. Knit a wider version for more coverage and a wider neckline, or a narrower version for a shorter, lighter accessory. The cast on end will be seamed to the side of the ribbing to create a round cowl neck. The shawl shaping is the same as in the narrower cowl, but the knitting continues so you can use most of your yarn.

TIP When wearing this shawl shape, I find it easiest to place the wider end/point first, then wrap the tail around my neck, once or twice depending on the length of the tail.

YARN

Fingering weight yarn in 2 contrasting colors

Cowl shown (page 113) in Hazel Knits Artisan Sock (90% Superwash Merino, 10% nylon; 400 yards/366 meters in 120 g), 1 skein each color Iris (DC) and Cackle (LC) | 180 yards/165 meters DC and 195 yards/178 meters LC for small cowl | 215 yards/197 meters DC and 230 yards/210 meters LC for large cowl

Shawl shown (page 111) in Hazel Knits Entice (70% Superwash Merino, 20% cashmere, 10% nylon; 400 yards/366 meters in 113 g), 1 skein each color Sapphire (DC) and Jellyfish (LC) | 400 yards/366 meters DC and 400 yards/366 meters LC

NEEDLES

Cowl: US 5/3.75 mm 24"/60 cm circular needle, or size to attain gauge or a fabric you like

Shawl: US 3/3.25 mm 24"/60 cm circular needle, or size to attain gauge or a fabric you like

GAUGE

Cowl: 19 sts in 4"/10 cm in Brioche Rib worked flat, before blocking | 17 sts in 4"/10 cm after blocking | Gauge not critical

Shawl: 24 sts in 4"/10 cm in Brioche Rib worked flat, before blocking | 19 sts in 4"/10 cm after blocking | Gauge not critical

Gauge is not critical for these pieces; cast on and knit a bit to see if you like your fabric. You're starting at the narrow end, so it makes a perfect gauge swatch. I used very different needles for these two yarns, which are both 400 yard/366 meter skeins with slightly different weights. Let your yarn be your guide.

NOTIONS

Tapestry needle
Stitch marker to indicate syncopation point

FINISHED SIZE

Small Cowl: 24"/61 cm at neck, 16"/40.5 cm along bound off edge, 15"/38 cm deep from neck edge to point C (diagonal line)

Large Cowl: 28"/71 cm at neck, 20"/51 cm along bound off edge, 17"/43 cm deep from neck edge to point C (diagonal line)

Shawl: 60"/152 cm long at neck, 28"/71 cm wide along bound off edge, 22"/56 cm deep from neck edge to point C (same shaping as Small Cowl, but elongated)

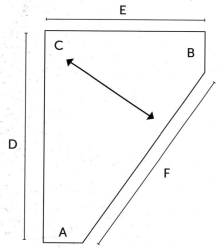

Small and large cowl measurements before blocking
A. Cast on 5"/13 cm
B. 5"/13 cm
C. Point
D. 26"/66 cm
E. Bind off edge 15"/38 cm (small); 20"/51 cm (large)
F. Neck edge 21"/53 cm (small); 24"/61 cm (large)

DIRECTIONS

With LC, CO 23 sts using Long Tail Cast On. Work Coffee Breakers pattern from written instructions or chart. Note: In the DC Brioche Rib section, stitches are increased on Rows 1 and 5 for the small cowl and shawl, and on Rows 1, 5, and 9 for the large cowl.

Setup Row LC (WS): (P1, sl1yo) 8x, p1, pm, (sl1yo, k1) 3x. Slide work back to beginning of row.

Setup Row DC (WS): Sl wyif, yb, (brk, sl1yo) 8x, sm, (brp, sl1yo) 2x, brp, yb, sl1 wyib. Turn work.

Row 1 LC (RS): P1, sl1yo, *brp, sl1yo; rep from * to m, sm, brkyobrk, (sl1yo, brk) 2x, sl1yo, brdecL, (sl1yo, brk) 3x, sl1yo, k1. Slide.

Row 1 DC (RS): Sl1 wyif, yb, brkyobrk, *sl1yo, brk; rep from * to m, sm, sl1yo, p1, (sl1yo, brp) 7x, yb, sl1 wyib. 2 sts inc in DC Brioche Rib section. Turn.

Row 2 LC (WS): P1, (sl1yo, brp) 8x, sm, *sl1yo, brk; rep from * to last 4 sts, (sl1yo, k1) 2x. Slide.

Row 2 DC (WS): Sl1 wyif, yb, (brk, sl1yo) 8x, sm, *brp, sl1yo; rep from * to last 2 sts, brp, yb, sl1 wyib. Turn.

Row 3 LC: P1, sl1yo, *brp, sl1yo; rep from * to m, sm, brk, sl1yo, brkyobrk, (sl1yo, brk) 2x, sl1yo, brdecL, (sl1yo, brk) 2x, sl1yo, k1. Slide.

Row 3 DC: Sl1 wyif, yb, brk, *sl1yo, brk; rep from * to m, sm, sl1yo, brp, sl1yo, p1, (sl1yo, brp) 6x, yb, sl1 wyib. Turn.

Row 4 LC: P1, (sl1yo, brp) 8x, sm, *sl1yo, brk; rep from * to last 2 sts, sl1yo, k1. Slide.

Row 4 DC: Sl1 wyif, yb, (brk, sl1yo) 8x, sm, *brp, sl1yo; rep from * to last 2 sts, brp, yb, sl1 wyib. Turn.

COFFEE BREAKERS CHART

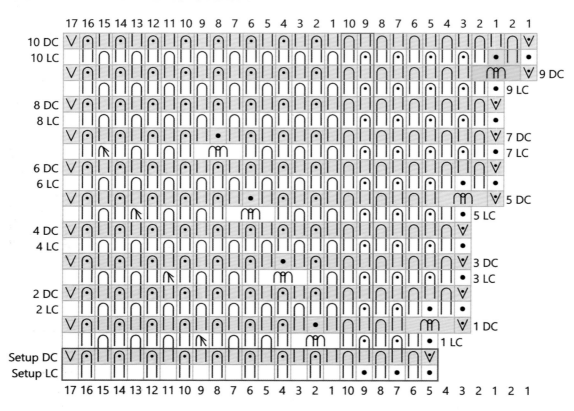

KEY

RS: knit / WS: purl	RS: purl / WS: knit	RS: brk / WS: brp
RS: brp / WS: brk	sl1yo	RS: brdecL
RS: brkyobrk	RS: slip purlwise wyif / WS: slip purlwise wyib	RS: slip purlwise wyib / WS: slip purlwise wyif
Large cowl only, work as brk for others	Large cowl only, omit for others	Setup Rows
DC Brioche Rib repeat	LC row	DC row

Row 5 LC: P1, sl1yo, *brp, sl1yo; rep from * to m, sm, (brk, sl1yo) 2x, brkyobrk, (sl1yo, brk) 2x, sl1yo, brdecL, sl1yo, brk, sl1yo, k1. Slide.

Row 5 DC: Sl1 wyif, yb, brkyobrk, *sl1yo, brk; rep from * to m, sm, (sl1yo, brp) 2x, sl1yo, p1, (sl1yo, brp) 5x, yb, sl1 wyib. 2 sts inc in DC Brioche Rib section. Turn.

Rows 6 LC & DC: Rep Rows 2 LC & DC.

Row 7 LC: P1, sl1yo, *brp, sl1yo; rep from * to m, sm, (brk, sl1yo) 3x, brkyobrk, (sl1yo, brk) 2x, sl1yo, brdecL, sl1yo, k1. Slide.

Row 7 DC: Sl1 wyif, yb, brk, *sl1yo, brk; rep from * to m, sm, (sl1yo, brp) 3x, sl1yo, p1, (sl1yo, brp) 4x, yb, sl1 wyib. Turn.

Rows 8 LC & DC: Rep Rows 4 LC & DC.

Row 9 LC: P1, sl1yo, *brp, sl1yo; rep from * to m, sm, (brk, sl1yo) 8x, k1. Slide.

Row 9 DC Small Cowl and Shawl only: Sl1 wyif, yb, brk, *sl1yo, brk; rep from * to m, sm, (sl1yo, brp) 8x, yb, sl1 wyib. Turn.

Row 9 DC Large Cowl only: Sl1 wyif, yb, brkyobrk, *sl1yo, brk; rep from * to m, sm, (sl1yo, brp) 8x, yb, sl1 wyib. 2 sts inc in DC Brioche Rib section. Turn.

Rows 10 LC & DC Small Cowl and Shawl only: Rep Rows 4 LC & DC.

Rows 10 LC & DC Large Cowl only: Rep Rows 2 LC & DC.

Coffee Breakers Cowl (small)

COWLS

Rep [Rows 1 LC & DC – 10 LC & DC] 11 more times; 120 rows worked from beginning. DC Brioche Rib increases complete.

Then work [Rows 1 LC & DC – 10 LC & DC] two times, but work DC Brioche Rib without increases on Rows 1 DC, 5 DC, (and 9 DC). This will create a flat seaming edge (edge B in schematic on page 110).

Go to Syncopated Ending.

SHAWL

Rep [Rows 1 LC & DC – 10 LC & DC] 26 more times (or to desired length); 270 rows worked from beginning.

Go to Syncopated Ending.

COFFEE BREAKERS LC BRIOCHE ENDING CHART

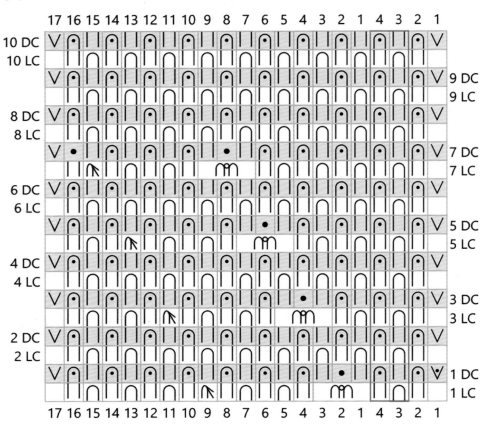

KEY

RS: knit / WS: purl	• RS: purl / WS: knit	∩ RS: brk / WS: brp
∩ RS: brp / WS: brk	‖ sl1yo	↑ RS: brdecL
ᵯ RS: brkyobrk	ⱴ RS: slip purlwise wyif / WS: slip purlwise wyib	V RS: slip purlwise wyib / WS: slip purlwise wyif
Large cowl only, work as brk for others	Large cowl only, omit for others	Setup Rows
DC Brioche Rib repeat	LC row	DC row

SYNCOPATED ENDING

The DC Brioche Rib section will be syncopated to become a LC Brioche Rib ending, matching the LC wave edging.

Work Coffee Breakers LC Brioche Ending pattern from written instructions or chart.

TIP Looking to maximize your yarn usage for your shawl? Weigh your yarns after each 10 row repeat, beginning after the 20th repeat. The grams per repeat will give you a good idea how many more repeats you can have in your shawl. The Syncopated Ending is also 10 rows, so leave enough for that last bit plus the bind off. Shawl shown has 28 repeats before the Syncopated Ending, and there were 3g DC and less than 1g LC left over. We love a good game of yarn chicken, when we can use a scale to tip the odds in our favor!

Row 1 LC (RS): K1, sl1yo, *brk, sl1yo; rep from * to m, sm, brkyobrk, (sl1yo, brk) 2x, sl1yo, brdecL, (sl1yo, brk) 3x, sl1yo, k1. Slide.

Row 1 DC (RS): Sl1 wyif, brp *sl1yo, brp; rep from * to m, sm, sl1yo, p1, (sl1yo, brp) 7x, yb, sl1 wyib. Turn.

Row 2 LC (WS): P1, *sl1yo, brp; rep from * to last 2 sts, sl1yo, p1. Slide.

Row 2 DC (WS): Sl1 wyif, yb, *brk, sl1yo; rep from * to last 2 sts, brk, yf, sl1 wyif. Turn.

Row 3 LC: K1, sl1yo, *brk, sl1yo; rep from * to m, sm, brk, sl1yo, brkyobrk, (sl1yo, brk) 2x, sl1yo, brdecL, (sl1yo, brk) 2x, sl1yo, k1. Slide.

Row 3 DC: Sl1 wyib, yf, brp, *sl1yo, brp; rep from * to m, sm, sl1yo, brp, sl1yo, p1, (sl1yo, brp) 6x, yb, sl1 wyib. Turn.

Rows 4 LC & DC: Rep Rows 2 LC & DC.

Row 5 LC: K1, sl1yo, *brk, sl1yo; rep from * to m, sm, (brk, sl1yo) 2x, brkyobrk, (sl1yo, brk) 2x, sl1yo, brdecL, sl1yo, brk, sl1yo, k1. Slide.

Row 5 DC: Sl1 wyib, yf, brp, *sl1yo, brp; rep from * to m, sm, (sl1yo, brp) 2x, sl1yo, p1, (sl1yo, brp) 5x, yb, sl1 wyib. Turn.

Rows 6 LC & DC: Rep Rows 2 LC & DC.

Row 7 LC: K1, sl1yo, *brk, sl1yo; rep from * to m, sm, (brk, sl1yo) 3x, brkyobrk, (sl1yo, brk) 2x, sl1yo, brdecL, sl1yo, k1. Slide.

Row 7 DC: Sl1 wyib, yf, brp, *sl1yo, brp; rep from * to m, sm, [(sl1yo, brp) 3x, sl1yo, p1] 2x, yb, sl1 wyib. Turn.

Rows 8 LC & DC: Rep Rows 2 LC & DC.

Row 9 LC: K1, sl1yo, *brk, sl1yo; rep from * to last st, k1. Slide.

Row 9 DC: Sl1 wyib, yf, brp, *sl1yo, brp; rep from * to last st, yb, sl1 wyib. Turn.

Rows 10 LC & DC: Repeat Rows 2 LC & DC.

Cut DC, leaving 6"/15 cm tail.

FINISHING

Closing Row LC (RS): K1, *p1, brk; rep from * to last 2 sts, p1, k1. Turn.

With WS facing, BO loosely in rib pattern using Jeny's Surprisingly Stretchy Bind Off. For cowl, cut 20"/51 cm tail for seaming. Sew in all ends (except the long LC tail for Cowl). Wet block to desired measurements.

For cowl, once dry: Thread tapestry needle with LC yarn tail. Seam CO edge to final 5"/12.5 cm of DC Brioche Rib edge (edge B). Sew in remaining tail.

CHAPTER 8

Fixing Mistakes

Sometimes things go wrong —it's true. Take a deep breath, and let's chat about how to recover.

FIXING A LOST YARN OVER

The most common mistake in brioche is a missing yarn over on your previous row/round's sl1yo when you go to brk or brp. There are only two places it could be: on the front of your work, or on the back of your work. Pick it up, and put it back on the needle with your stitch, making sure that the right leg is in front. This works on both brk and brp rounds.

TINKING YOUR STITCHES, OR UN-KNITTING

Tink is just the word knit, spelled backwards because going backwards, or unknitting, is exactly how you do it. You can undo your stitches, one by one, the same way you do in regular knitting. The only difference for brioche is that you need to make sure you get both **the stitch and the yarnover** back, as you undo the brk or brp stitch. To undo a sl1yo, slip the stitch back to the left needle, and let the yarn over fall away.

For a yo dropped at the back of your work

Dropped yo behind brk column (there should be only one dark strand behind the st, not two).

Pick up yo and place it on left needle with its stitch.

For a yo dropped at the front of your work

Dropped yo in front of brk column.

Slip st to right needle, pick up the yo.

Replace restored sl1yo to left needle.

THE PINCH, FOR TINKING DECREASES

To tink a brioche decrease, the easiest way is to pinch underneath the stitches so they can't run down. Slide the decrease off the needle, and gently pull the working yarn out of the decrease. Pick up the stitches and their associated yarn overs with your right needle tip. Don't worry if they're seated correctly; **catch the stitches first.** You can correct the stitch mount and pick up missing yarn overs as you move them back to the left needle after the stitches are secure. (You can also pinch/pull with the opposite hand, and pick up stitches with your left needle tip.)

Pinch, and slide decrease off needle.

Pull yarn from decrease.

Pick up the stitches and the associated yos, then move sts back to left needle.

CHAPTER 9

Special Techniques

BLOCKING YOUR BRIOCHE

Just about any kind of knitting can benefit from blocking when you're finished with it. Blocking helps even out your stitches, and it sets your stitches into fabric. If you want to keep the bouncy squish of your brioche fabric, steam blocking is best. (I generally steam block most of my brioche accessories.) Be forewarned, when the pieces eventually do need washing, they'll come out a bit flatter. Be very gentle — don't stretch — and push the fabric back to its original shape.

I prefer to wet block my shawls and other fingering weight projects because there's a lot of leeway when it comes to brioche. Soak your knit for 20 minutes or longer in tepid water with a bit of no-rinse wool wash. Drain, and gently squeeze out the excess water. Roll your project in a folded towel and walk on it. (Really!) Repeat the roll and walk once or twice, then lay it out to dry. Note that wet brioche is *very* stretchy! Don't be alarmed. If you're not pinning the fabric out to train it in a larger shape, it will bounce back a bit when it's dry, especially if it's superwash wool. Coffee Bean Trivia (page 101) and Coffee Breakers (page 107) are examples of pieces where I've gently laid out the wet pieces without stretching them. If you want your piece to hold a larger shape, as in the Seagull Flight shawl, pin it out to your desired dimensions and let it dry completely before unpinning it.

LONG TAIL CAST ON

The trick to a successful Long Tail Cast On for brioche or any other knitting is to make sure that there is space between the stitches when casting on. Use your finger to keep a space while adding the next stitch; this prevents the edge from being too tight for the extra stretchy/squishy brioche fabric. The Long Tail Cast On is my go-to cast on, but you can use any cast on you like, as long as you can leave a little space between your stitches.

SUSPENDED BIND OFF

Work 2 sts, but do not drop the second stitch from left needle. With your left needle, lift the right stitch on the right needle over the left stitch and off the right needle (as in a standard bind off). Then, finish dropping the second stitch from left needle. *Work next st, but do not drop stitch from left needle. With left needle, lift right stitch on right needle over left stitch and off right needle, and THEN finish dropping stitch from left needle. Rep from * until all sts have been worked. Fasten off, sew in ends. See Resources on page 121 for more information.

JENY'S SURPRISINGLY STRETCHY BIND OFF

This bind off is very stretchy, due to added yarn overs. When binding off, add a reverse yo before each knit st, and a standard yo before each purl st. The yo is passed over and off with the preceding st. **Example:** P1, *reverse yo, k1, pass yo and previous purl st over k1, yo, p1, pass yo and previous knit st over p1; rep from * to end. See Resources on page 121 for more information.

Iced Latte Cowl. See page 30 for pattern.

Abbreviations

BO – Bind off

BOR – Beginning of round

brdecL – Brioche left leaning double decrease, tutorial on page 50-51

brdecR – Brioche right leaning double decrease, tutorial on page 52-53

brk – Brioche knit: Knit stitch with its paired yo

brk2tog – Brioche knit 2 together: Brioche knit the next purl st together with the following sl1yo (1 st decrease)

brp – Brioche purl: Purl stitch with its paired yo

brkyobrk – Brk, yo, brk, all in next st (2 st increase)

br4st dec – Brioche 4 st decrease, tutorial on page 56-58

br4st inc – Brk, yo, brk, yo, brk, all in the next st (4 st increase)

bruwdec – Brioche unwrapped double decrease, tutorial on page 54-55

CC – Contrast color

CO – Cast on

DC – Dark color

dec – Decrease

dpns – Double pointed needles

inc – Increase

k – Knit

k2tog – Knit 2 together; one st decreased

kfb – Knit in front and back of st; one st increased

LC – Light color

m – Marker

MC – Main color

p – Purl

p2tog – Purl 2 together

pm – Place marker

rem – Remain

rnd, rnds – Round, rounds

RS – Right side

sl – Slip stitch, purlwise unless otherwise instructed

sl1 wyib – Slip 1 st purlwise with yarn in back

sl1 wyif – Slip 1 st purlwise with yarn in front

sl1yo – Slipped st with paired yarnover

sm – Slip marker

st, sts – Stitch, stitches

WS – Wrong side

yo – Yarn over

yf, yb – Yarn forward, yarn back. Move yarn to front or back between needles.

Italian Soda Cowl. See page 34 for pattern.

Resources

HAZEL KNITS
Seattle, Washington (USA)
hazelknits.com

HUCKLEBERRY KNITS
Bellingham, Washington (USA)
huckleberryknits.com

KNIT PICKS
Vancouver, Washington (USA)
knitpicks.com

MALABRIGO
Montevideo, (Uruguay)
malabrigoyarn.com

PDXKNITTERATI
my blog, tutorials, resources for this book (including video tutorials)

pdxknitterati.com

pdxknitterati.com/tutorials/

pdxknitterati.com/brioche-knit-love-book-resources/

Acknowledgements

Marie Greene, founder of Library House Press, asked me if I thought I had a book in me. Why yes, I guess I did! Thank you to Marie Greene and Carlee Wright for guiding me through the process. Thanks also to Meaghan Schmaltz, my excellent tech editor since long before this book, and Angela Watts for the beautiful photography. It takes a village to make a book, and that village includes test knitters all over the world. Thank you test knitters, and especially Ann Berg, sample knitter extraordinaire. Thank you to my lovely sister, Sharon Lee Hsu, for modeling my knits with me! Special thanks to Hazel Knits, Knit Picks, and Malabrigo for the beautiful yarn they provided for the samples for this book. Thank you to Nancy Marchant for sharing brioche with the knitting world; her stitch patterns in *Knitting Fresh Brioche* are a great design resource.

Thank you to my husband Phil, who is my biggest fan, and he doesn't even knit! His love and support (and mad take-out skillz) made this book possible. Thanks to my sons, Tyler and Ryan, who did learn how to knit. Fond thanks and love to my Aunt Rose for teaching me to knit, oh so long ago. And thank you to the knitters who create such beautiful things with sticks and string.

Coffee Breakers Shawl. See page 107 for pattern.

Thank You

Thank you to the many test knitters who made this book possible, and a very special thank you to Ann Berg. Ann has been test knitting for me since I met her when I taught at the Sheeper Than Therapy Guild Retreat in 2016. She volunteered to knit samples for this book when I developed forearm tendonitis (take breaks from your knitting, please!). She knit the Iced Latte Cowl, Iced Latte Hat, Berry Galette Cowl, Green Tea Chai, large Coffee Breakers Cowl, and Coffee Breakers Shawl.

Ann Berg	Kathy Green	Melissa A. Rowe
Audrey Blankenship	Michelle Jernstedt	Kimberly Roy
Cate Campbell	Katie Marsh	Gwen Schweitzer
Jan Cornelius	Savannah Maughan	Susan Shepperd
Selena Croxall	Cathleen McMahon	Leslie Singer
Giovanna Cracchiolo	Terri Miles	Amanda Smith
Katie Daugherty	Lynn Murphy	Jaime Smith
Karen des Jardins	Patricia Ann O'Connor	Chelsea Steele
Megan Drake	Stephanie Pinkney	Jae Tauber
Marie Ferner	Blythe Polreis	Eileen Westenberg
Edana French	Kris Redmond	Anita Williams
Elsbeth Grant	Heather Roach	

About the Author

Michele Lee Bernstein is PDXKnitterati. (PDX is the airport code for Portland, Oregon.) She specializes in designing accessories, especially when they use one or two skeins of very special yarn. She's fond of texture (brioche, lace, entrelac, elongated stitches) and loves the way techniques can be used to make small projects sing. Brioche has been her favorite technique since 2017. Her patterns are available through Ravelry, Payhip, Knit Picks, and Love Crafts.

Michele loves teaching knitters to be the boss of their knitting! She teaches at local yarn shops, fiber festivals (Red Alder Fiber Arts Festival, Oregon Flock and Fiber Festival, Vogue Knitting Live), and retreats, as well as remotely via Zoom for Virtual Knitting Live and local yarn shops.

Michele blogs about knitting, food, and music at PDXKnitterati.com. You can also find her on Instagram, Facebook, Ravelry, and YouTube; she's PDXKnitterati on all platforms. Subscribe to her mailing list at http://eepurl.com/cniNPX for knitting news, techniques, and special offers on newly released designs.

Michele lives in Portland, Oregon, with her husband Phil, and cats Biscuit and Calvin, aka StrikeForce!

Index

A

abbreviations, 119

Aran weight yarn, Hello Brioche Hat, 19-20

B

basic stitches, 10-14

Berry Galette Cowl, 64-67

Berry Galette Wristlets, 68-71

bind off/binding off, 117

    Jeny's Surprisingly Stretchy, 117

    suspended, 117

blocking, 117

bottom up

    Berry Galette Cowl, 64-67

    Crema Cowl, 40-42

    Hello Brioche Hat, 19-20

    Iced Latte Cowl, 30-32

    Iced Latte Hat, 60-63

    Peppermint Mocha Cup Cozy, 28-29

    Peppermint Mocha Coaster, 37-38

br4st dec, 56-58

br4st inc, 50

brdecL, 50-51

brdecR, 52-53

brioche rib

    Hello Brioche Hat, 19-20

    Hello Brioche Mitts, 21-22

    Hello Brioche Scarf, 16-18

    Grande Brioche Cowl, 26-27

brioche stockinette

    Peppermint Mocha Cup Cozy, 28-29

brk, 10

brk2tog, 119

brkyobrk, 49

brp, 10

bruwdec, 54-55

button band, Italian Soda Cowl, 34-36

buttons, Italian Soda Cowl, 34-36

C

Cappuccino Cowl, 85-89

cast on/casting on, 117

    long tail, 117

charts, how to read, 39, 58

charts, patterns with

    Latte Leaf Coaster and Cup Cozy, 76-83

    Berry Galette Cowl, 64-67

    Berry Galette Wristlets, 68-71

    Cappuccino Cowl, 85-89

    Coffee Bean Trivia Cowl, 101-106

    Coffee Breakers Cowl/Shawl, 107-113

    Green Tea Chai Scarf, 72-75

    Iced Latte Cowl, 30-32

    Iced Latte Hat, 60-63

    Seafoam Latte Scarf, 90-93

    Seagull Flight Shawl, 94-100

    Shortbread Scarf, 43-46

coasters
    Latte Leaf Coaster, 76-80
    Peppermint Mocha Coaster, 37-38
Coffee Bean Trivia Cowl, 101-106
Coffee Breakers Cowl/Shawl, 107-113
cowl
    Berry Galette Cowl, 64-67
    Cappuccino Cowl, 85-89
    Coffee Bean Trivia Cowl, 101-106
    Coffee Breakers Cowl/Shawl, 107-113
    Crema Cowl, 40-42
    Grande Brioche Cowl, 26-27
    Iced Latte Cowl, 30-32
    Italian Soda Cowl, 34-36
Crema Cowl, 40-42
cup cozy
    Latte Leaf Cup Cozy, 77, 82-83
    Peppermint Mocha Cup Cozy, 28-29

D
decreases/decreasing, 48, 50-58
DK weight Yarn
    Iced Latte Cowl, 30-32
    Iced Latte Hat, 60-63

F
Fingering weight yarn
    Coffee Bean Trivia Cowl, 101-106
    Coffee Breakers Cowl/Shawl, 107-113
    Seagull Flight Shawl, 94-100

fixing mistakes, 114-116

G
gauge, 9
Grande Brioche Cowl, 26-27
Green Tea Chai Scarf, 72-75

H
hat
    Hello Brioche Hat, 19-20
    Iced Latte Hat, 60-63
Hello Brioche Hat, 19-20
Hello Brioche Mitts, 21-22
Hello Brioche Scarf, 16-18

I
Iced Latte Cowl, 30-32
Iced Latte Hat, 60-63
increases/increasing, 48-50
Italian Soda Cowl, 34-36

J
Jeny's Surprisingly Stretchy Bind-Off, 117

K
knit, flat
    Hello Brioche Scarf, 16-18
    Italian Soda Cowl, 34-36
knitting resources, 121

L
Latte Leaf Coaster & Cup Cozy, 76-83
Long Tail Cast On, 117

M

mistakes, fixing, 114-116

mitts, Hello Brioche Mitts, 21-22

N

needles, 9

O

one-color brioche knitting, 15

one-color

Hello Brioche Hat, 19-20

Hello Brioche Mitts, 21-22

Hello Brioche Scarf, 16-18

P

Peppermint Mocha Coaster, 37-38

Peppermint Mocha Cup Cozy, 28-29

R

reading charts, 39, 58

recipe, Chocolate Chip Shortbread, 47

resources, 121

Round, patterns in the

Berry Galette Cowl, 64-67

Hello Brioche Hat, 19-20

Cappuccino Cowl, 85-89

Grande Brioche Cowl, 26-27

Iced Latte Cowl, 30-32

Iced Latte Hat, 60-63

Peppermint Mocha Cup Cozy, 28-29

Row/Round numbers, 39

S

scarf

Green Tea Chai Scarf, 72-75

Hello Brioche Scarf, 16-18

Seafoam Latte Scarf, 90-93

Shortbread Scarf, 43-46

Seagull Flight Shawl, 94-100

shawl

Coffee Breakers Cowl/Shawl, 107-113

Seagull Flight Shawl, 94-100

Shortbread Scarf, 43-46

sl1yo, 11, 15

sl1yo-BRK, 11, 13

sl1yo-BRP, 12, 14

special techniques, 117

super bulky weight yarn, Hello Brioche Scarf, 16-18

supplies, 9

suspended bind off, 117

syncopated brioche, 39

Cappuccino Cowl, 85-89

Coffee Bean Trivia Cowl, 101-106

Coffee Breakers Cowl/Shawl, 107-113

Crema Cowl, 40-42

Latte Leaf Coaster & Cup Cozy, 76-83

Seafoam Latte Scarf, 90-93

Seagull Flight Shawl, 94-100

Shortbread Scarf, 43-46

T

techniques, 10-14, 49-58, 114-116, 117

tinking, 114, 116

tinking, decreases, 116

tutorials, 10-14, 48-58, 114-116

two-color

    Berry Galette Cowl, 64-67

    Berry Galette Wristlets, 68-71

    Cappuccino Cowl, 85-89

    Coffee Bean Trivia Cowl, 101-106

    Coffee Breakers Cowl/Shawl, 107-113

    Crema Cowl, 40-42

    Grande Brioche Cowl, 26-27

    Green Tea Chai Scarf, 72-75

    Iced Latte Cowl, 30-32

    Iced Latte Hat, 60-63

    Italian Soda Cowl, 34-36

    Latte Leaf Coaster and Cup Cozy, 76-83

    Peppermint Mocha Coaster, 37-38

    Peppermint Mocha Cup Cozy, 28-29

    Seafoam Latte Scarf, 90-93

    Seagull Flight Shawl, 94-100

    Shortbread Scarf, 43-46

two-color, flat, 33

two-color, round, 23

W

Worsted weight yarn

    Berry Galette Cowl, 64-67

    Berry Galette Wristlets, 68-71

    Cappuccino Cowl, 85-89

    Crema Cowl, 40-42

    Grande Brioche Cowl, 26-27

    Green Tea Chai Scarf, 72-75

    Hello Brioche Hat, 19-20

    Hello Brioche Mitts, 21-22

    Italian Soda Cowl, 34-36

    Latte Leaf Coaster and Cup Cozy, 76-83

    Peppermint Mocha Coaster, 37-38

    Peppermint Mocha Cup Cozy, 28-29

    Seafoam Latte Scarf, 90-93

    Shortbread Scarf, 43-46

wristlets, Berry Galette Wristlets, 68-71

Y

yarn over, fixing a lost yo, 114-115

Thank you for purchasing this book and supporting an independent publisher.

Library House Press